"Whether you are studying this book as part of a small group experience, or the two of you are simply working through it as husband and wife, you will discover not only the tools, but also the knowledge of how to use those tools to build a great marriage. The dreams you had when you said, *I do,* can become reality when you apply the insights provided in *Tools for a Great Marriage*."

> Gary D. Chapman, PhD
> Author of *The Five Love Languages* and
> *The Five Languages of Apology*

"In *Tools for a Great Marriage,* Willie Batson gives you the blueprint for building your marriage on God's principles in a format that is simple, clear, practical, and easy to apply. This is a book that husbands will enjoy reading. Follow-up questions set the stage for great couple's times together. We've known Willie and Cindy for many years and can say without any reservations, they live out the message of this book in their own marriage. We highly recommend that you put *Tools for a Great Marriage* on the top of your reading (and doing) list!"

> Claudia & David Arp, MSW
> Authors of the *10 Great Dates*® series and *The Second Half of Marriage*

Tools for a Great Marriage

Tools for a Great Marriage

PRACTICAL HELP FOR BUILDING A MARRIAGE THAT LASTS

WILLIAM BATSON

FAMILY BUILDERS MINISTRIES

Tools for a Great Marriage
William Batson
Copyright © 2008 William Batson

First Printing – June 2008
Second Printing – May 2009

ISBN-13: 978-0-9816816-0-3
ISBN-10: 0-9816816-0-3

Publisher Information:

Family Builders Ministries, Inc.
PO Box 274
Cape Neddick, ME 03902-0274
207.361.1030

Find more information on the web: www.familybuilders.net

Where it was deemed appropriate, the author has changed the names and other identifying information of couples whose stories appear in this book.

Printed in the United States of America

Mixed Sources
Product group from well-managed forests and other controlled sources
www.fsc.org Cert no. SW-COC-002283
© 1996 Forest Stewardship Council
FSC

Dedicated to

Cindy,
the one my heart loves.

CONTENTS

Resources

ACKNOWLEDGEMENTS

I am indebted to many people who have influenced the content and structure of this book. They shared their thoughts, suggestions, and time, to make this an effective tool for married couples. I hope they are pleased.

I will be forever grateful to the couples in our Tuesday night small group – Glenn and Marilyn Page, Alan and Suzan Michaud, Don and Jackie Mercier, and Wes and Lisa Mills – who met over a period of several weeks to review the early versions of the manuscript and try out the *Tool Time for Couples* exercises. Their suggestions and feedback significantly influenced the final version that you are reading.

David Squire and Carol Arnold helped me fine-tune the early manuscript. Their attention to grammar and punctuation, and the suggestions regarding content, were right on the mark. I also want to thank Ed Stuart, whose constructive review of the manuscript motivated me to produce a book that I think is much better than originally designed.

I want to acknowledge the Board of Directors of Family Builders

Ministries for their support during this project – Jack Richardson, Les and Eunice Hanscom, Jere Vincent, David and Jean Squire, Scott Keith, and Cindy Batson. They each have a heart for this ministry and for the building of great marriages and families.

I also want to acknowledge my daughters and their husbands – Courtney and Erik Pedersen, Cammie and David Gilchrist – for the opportunity to create *The Family Builders' Tool Bag* for their weddings. They also helped with the book cover design. Lisa Baker is due recognition for the original idea of the marital tool bag and Doug Tappan helped to make the cover copy sharp and relevant.

Where would this book be without the enduring support and invaluable help of my wife, Cindy? Her belief in the value of this project made me want to finish it, when it would have been so easy to walk away from it. She sacrificed hours, even days, so that I could write and rewrite the manuscript, and patiently let me talk about this book in just about every conversation we had. She lovingly and painstakingly invested her editorial talents in the final manuscript, for which I am eternally grateful. Now we can spend some quality time together.

Finally, I want to thank all of the couples who attended our marriage conferences and seminars over the past 22 years. Their enthusiasm inspires us to continue building great marriages and families from generation to generation.

To God be the glory!

How to Use This Book

Intellectual exposure to truth bears little fruit in your marriage; however, the practical and daily application of that truth in your marriage reaps a bountiful harvest. With that in mind, you will find opportunities to interact with the material throughout this book called, *Tool Time for Couples*. You and your spouse will gain more from this book by reading it together, discussing your answers to the questions, and completing the projects. I suggest you read one chapter per week, setting aside a regular time to meet together for discussion.

Tools for a Great Marriage is an excellent resource for a couples' small group or class. I have produced a leader's manual to help you conduct the group meetings, and guide the discussions. You can download this free resource from our website.

I want to know how *Tools for a Great Marriage* helps you improve your marriage. A special page has been set up on our website for you to post your story (www.familybuilders.net). I look forward to hearing from you.

FOREWORD

When most couples get married, they fully intend to have a great marriage. They have visions of making each other supremely happy. The great tragedy of this generation is that over half of these couples will have their dreams shattered by divorce. The reality is that great marriages do not simply appear on the horizon of life after the wedding ceremony. Great marriages must be constructed by husbands and wives working together as a team.

I once attempted to build a tree house for my children. However, because I didn't have the proper tools and didn't have the architectural knowledge, my tree house turned out to look more like a ladder leading to nowhere. My desire to construct a tree house was not sufficient to bring the project to reality. I solicited the help of my neighbor. With his tools and expertise, we were able to accomplish my dream.

Couples often come to marriage with few relationship tools and little knowledge of how to build a mutually satisfying marriage. In this book, William Batson not only supplies the tools, but also gives you the instructions on how to use them to create a truly great marriage. It will still require time and effort on your part, but at least your efforts will be directed toward accomplishing your dream of a great marriage.

Willie Batson is not a novice in the marriage building business. For over twenty years, he has been helping churches establish marriage and family ministries for their communities. Willie and Cindy have been married for 35 years and raised two beautiful daughters, who are now in the process of building their own great marriages. I met Willie over 10 years ago as he drove me from the Boston airport to Worcester, Massachusetts for a conference. Before the ride was over, I realized that I had discovered a fellow marriage builder who had a desire to see marriages thrive, and to see churches lead the way in marriage enrichment. We both agreed that the only hope for restoring the sanctity of marriage in western culture is for churches, of all sizes, to provide ongoing marital enrichment programs. I believe that this book, *Tools for a Great Marriage*, is an excellent resource for churches who are trying to offer couples practical, Biblical guidance in building strong marriages.

Whether you are studying this book as part of a small group experience, or the two of you are simply working through it as husband and wife, you will discover not only the tools, but also the knowledge of how to use those tools to build a great marriage. The dreams you had when you said, "I do," can become reality when you apply the insights provided in *Tools for a Great Marriage*.

Gary D. Chapman, PhD
Winston-Salem, NC
Author of *The Five Love Languages* and
The Five Languages of Apology

A Great Marriage Tool Bag

What do you give your daughter and her husband on their wedding day? Do you give them an all-expense-paid honeymoon on some romantic island, or a set of table trays? Do you give them a new house, or a lifetime membership at the local gym?

That was on my mind as I pondered what I would say at the weddings of each of our daughters. Since I am an ordained minister, they had asked me to perform their marriage ceremonies. I wanted a creative way to challenge them to build a great marriage. A friend suggested I give them a tool bag. Immediately, my creativity cells kicked into gear, and I decided to give them what we called *The Family Builders' Tool Bag*. The concept was that just as you need tools to build and maintain a house, a couple needs certain tools for building and maintaining a great marriage.

I bought a tool bag, packed it with tools, and presented it to them during their wedding ceremonies. The tools would come in handy around the house and would serve to remind them of what is necessary for building a lasting marriage. I didn't reveal all of the tools at the ceremony, only a few key ones. Let me tell you how they relate to building a great marriage.

A BIBLE

The first one was not your typical household tool. It was a Bible, which is like the foundation upon which you build your house. You cannot just arrive at a building lot, pull out your hammer and some nails, and start putting up walls. I guess you could, but you might not like the results. You need a sturdy and reliable foundation upon which to construct that house.

The Word of God is foundational to building a marriage that is strong, durable, and lasting.

The Word of God is foundational to building a marriage that is strong, durable, and lasting. The Apostle Paul wrote that all of the Bible "is inspired by God and is useful to teach us what is true and to make us realize what is wrong in our lives. It straightens us out and teaches us to do what is right. It is God's way of preparing us in every way, fully equipped for every good thing God wants us to do" (2 Timothy 3:16, NLT). As an example, God's Word is an authoritative resource in teaching us how to get along with others. Just consider the following verses for example:

> *Be kind and compassionate to one another, forgiving each other, just as in Christ God forgave you. – Ephesians 4:32*

Don't grumble against each other, brothers, or you will be judged. The Judge is standing at the door! – James 5:9

Do not lie to each other, since you have taken off your old self with its practices. – Colossians 3:9

Therefore, confess your sins to each other and pray for each other so that you may be healed. The prayer of a righteous man is powerful and effective. – James 5:16

And let us consider how we may spur one another on toward love and good deeds. – Hebrews 10:24

Love each other with genuine affection, and take delight in honoring each other. – Romans 12:10, NLT

Imagine the kind of marriage you would have if you both practiced these guidelines – a great marriage!

AN ADJUSTABLE WRENCH

The next thing I pulled out of the tool bag was an adjustable wrench. To succeed in marriage you must be able to adjust to each other's unique personalities and opinions. I remember reading about two porcupines in Alaska that kept warm by cuddling together. Because their quills pricked each other, they moved apart. Soon they were shivering again, and had to cuddle for their own survival. They needed each other, even though they *needled* each other! (I love corny humor.) The only way they were able to survive was by continually adjusting their quills.

Adjusting to each other does not mean you have to fully understand your spouse. I will never understand how Cindy, my wife, can adoringly hold a mouse in her hands, but let out the most horrific scream when she sees a spider on the other side of the room. She will never understand why I don't enjoy swimming as much as she does.

A spouse's willingness to adjust comes from a heart that is grateful for the strengths that exist, rather than frustrated by what is missing. It can be difficult at times to accept your spouse with all of his or her unique and individual traits. When you think about it, those are probably the very attributes that first attracted you to each other. Making adjustments in your attitude about your spouse will result in respect and thanksgiving.

A SET OF CLAMPS

After the wrench, I pulled out a set of clamps, the kind used to hold pieces of wood together. They represent those times when you need to *clamp* your mouth shut to avoid saying things that will be harmful. The Bible advises us to avoid using "foul or abusive language. Let everything you say be good and helpful, so that your words will be an encouragement to those who hear them" (Ephesians 4:29, NLT).

Your words can bring either life or death to your marriage.

Words are powerful. Your words can bring either life or death to your marriage. Before you speak, it is wise to ask, *Will this be helpful or hurtful?* I am not saying that we should avoid important issues that every married couple must face, but we are to be wise in how we navigate those minefields. The Bible says, "Even a fool is thought wise if he keeps silent, and discerning if he holds his tongue" (Proverbs 17:28).

A HATCHET

Next, I pulled out a hatchet. This tool represents forgiveness, as in, "Let's bury the hatchet," a saying from a Native American Indian ritual for sealing a peace treaty. When two warring tribes ended a conflict, they would dig a hole in the ground to bury a hatchet as a symbol of peace, and as a promise not to attack each other in the future.

Forgiveness is not easy for many couples because of what is expected of them. According to David W. Augsburger, forgiveness is costly in marriage for the following reasons:

- *It means accepting instead of demanding repayment for the wrong done.*

- *It means releasing the other instead of exacting revenge.*

- *It means reaching out in love instead of relinquishing resentments.* [1]

Forgiveness may seem like an unnatural act, but it is a most powerful tool for keeping your marriage strong and moving in the right direction.

A CAN OF WD-40

The next item I pulled out of the tool bag was a can of WD-40, something many of us use around the house to keep things working smoothly. The intent of this tool was to remind them that healthy communication keeps a marriage working easily and efficiently. The side of the can lists these features of the product:

- *Stops Squeaks*

- *Cleans and Protects*

- *Loosens Rusted Parts*

- *Frees Sticky Mechanisms*

A married couple who knows how to communicate well is able to drive out the things that can cause their relationship to deteriorate and shut down.

With that I closed the bag, pronounced them husband and wife, and sent them on their way to begin building their own great marriages.

YOUR GREAT MARRIAGE TOOL BAG

Every couple enters marriage with their own bag of tools, but many are frustrated by their attempts at fixing things. They either have the wrong tools or do not use the tools properly. Having the right tools in your marital tool bag and using them properly will help you build and sustain a great marriage. I know the positive and lasting results of using the right tools in the right way. I want you to experience the same thing.

> *Having the right tools in your marital tool bag and using them properly will help you build and sustain a great marriage.*

On an airplane somewhere over the northeastern part of the United States, the passenger next to me initiated a conversation. It was soon apparent that we had some striking differences in life experience. He had been married and divorced, was a recovering alcoholic, played in a funk music band, taught piano, and was on his way to a Stevie Wonder concert. Our spirited conversation took more twists and turns than did our airplane that day. When he discovered that I was a marriage educator, nothing hindered him from telling me about the lessons he had learned from his past and present relationships.

His most profound statement related to something he tells his piano students, "Practice makes perfect. But, if you practice wrong, you will be perfectly wrong." Immediately, I thought of the couples who practice wrong relational skills repeatedly. They escalate arguments in order to intimidate and demean each other. They readily point out the flaws of loved ones and ignore their own serious deficiencies. Doing the same thing so many times and for so long, they become experts in being perfectly wrong. Practice is important, but my new friend taught me that the *way* we practice is much more fundamental to success. Our tools and methods must be grounded in the counsel of God, who designed marriage. Otherwise, they lack the power to sustain a lasting and fulfilling relationship as God intended.

A SPECIAL WORD

I realize that some people who read this book have been previously married. If you fall into that category, some of what I say may create a little pinch in your spirit. It is not my intent to heap loads of guilt upon you for what happened, or did not happen, in a prior marriage. I want to help you with tools that can make this marriage strong, healthy, and lasting. I hope I am successful.

A GREAT MARRIAGE IS NOT AUTOMATIC

A great marriage is not automatic. It is the result of one man and one woman fully committed to each other and to God's plan of a lifetime together. It takes two people who are willing to do the required work because they know their marriage is worth it.

Do you want a great marriage? Most people do. Yet, few people have great marriages, in large part, because it is so easy to settle for the mundane in marriage. I'm sure that *mundane* is not a word you want associated with your marriage. I doubt you started out with the goal of having a mundane marriage, but it can happen. You get stuck in the routine busyness of doing life together. Work and kids get the bulk of your energy and time. You lose your sense of adventure and settle for what is safe. As long as you sleep in the same bed, don't fight, go to your kid's games, and pay your bills, then it must be good. You know your roles. You take out the trash. Your spouse makes breakfast. You keep the social calendar. Your spouse does the banking. You're comfortable. It's a *good* marriage, but it's not *great*.

I'm not against good marriages. They are better than bad marriages. However, I do not think God intended for marriage to become mundane or boring. One of the ways your good marriage can become a great marriage is by filling your marital tool bag with the right tools and tossing out the ones that are not working. That's where this book can help you. As you read the remaining chapters, may God give you courage to do what will help you build a great marriage that lasts.

 TOOL TIME FOR COUPLES

1. Successfully completing this book as a couple requires a regular time together for reading and/or discussing the material. Some couples like to take turns reading the material aloud to each other and discussing it. Others prefer reading it separately and meeting to discuss their thoughts and reactions. It does not matter which way you do it, as long as you do it. Decide now when and how you will use this book to improve your marriage.

2. Before moving on to the next chapter, take the opportunity to evaluate your relationship. In the Resource Section, you will find an exercise called, *Your Marriage Checkup*. There is one for each of you. Complete the checkup, including the discussion section, in order to know what your strength and growth areas are at this time. When you have finished the book and completed the *Tool Time* exercises in each chapter, repeat the checkup with a different colored pen. Note how you have increased or not increased your level of satisfaction in the various categories and discuss the reasons why. What do you still need to work on?

CHAPTER *2*

Building on a
Great Foundation

The men who poured the foundation for our house learned a valuable lesson. Before starting on ours, they had put in a foundation
for another house in town. It did not meet the local code requirements
regarding the amount of rebar – the steel bars used to reinforce the
poured concrete in the foundation. The building code officer made the
contractor remove the foundation and put in one that met town stan-
dards. That was an expensive lesson to learn.

The type of foundation upon which we build our marriages is just
as critical. Jesus taught the importance of building on a solid foundation in this parable:

> *Anyone who listens to my teaching and obeys me is wise,*
> *like a person who builds a house on solid rock. Though the*

rain comes in torrents and the floodwaters rise and the winds beat against that house, it won't collapse, because it is built on rock. But anyone who hears my teaching and ignores it is foolish, like a person who builds a house on sand. When the rains and floods come and the winds beat against that house, it will fall with a mighty crash. – Matthew 7:24-27, NLT

A marriage based on ever-changing emotions and ideas is similar to a house built on shifting sand. It's foolish and leads to short-term solutions. Wise couples build their marriages on the unchanging, rock-solid foundation of God's Word. Jesus says the wise person not only hears his word, but also obeys it. The foolish person is the one who ignores what God says about marital behavior.

Jesus' story about the wise and foolish builders reminds me of two lighthouses built on the eastern shore of the United States. On the rocky coast of Maine, the Nubble Light stands upon a massive rock jutting out into the Atlantic Ocean. For more than 125 years, it has withstood the howling winds and surging waves of New England storms. For me, it symbolizes the strength and endurance of building a marriage in such a way that it is strong from the very start. It is less costly, in many ways, to build on a solid foundation, using the right tools and materials. Couples whose marriages endure the waves that crash around and upon them will be a beacon of strength and hope for others.

Another lighthouse stands on the shifting sands of coastal North Carolina. The Cape Hatteras Lighthouse was built in 1870 on the barrier islands known as the Outer Banks. However, a little more than a hundred years later it was in peril because of the erosion of the beach by turbulent storms and tides. Originally built 1,600 feet from the sea, it was now only 160 feet from collapsing into the invading waves of the Atlantic Ocean. Concerned citizens launched a massive effort to save the lighthouse by relocating it a half-mile from its original site. The rescuers of the Cape Hatteras Lighthouse waited almost too long in their efforts to save it. Had it been built on a more solid foundation, a lot of money, time, and energy would have been saved.

The Bible, God's Word, is the spiritual foundation upon which to build a great marriage. As you read and listen to its wisdom, putting into practice what you learn, you will establish a rock solid spiritual foundation. Here's a note from a wife who attributes the strength of her marriage to a Godly foundation:

> *I consider myself blessed to have such a passionate relationship with my husband after 19 years of ups and downs. I would never change a single thing, always placing our Heavenly Father at the center of our marriage, including him in every decision we make in our lives.*

How do you build a great spiritual foundation for your marriage? Just as my town requires a minimum amount of rebar in the concrete to assure a strong foundation, there are some minimal requirements for a spiritual foundation in your marriage.

FAITH IN GOD

Faith in a personal God who loves you and is concerned for your well-being is fundamental to building a great marriage. I'm not talking about accepting a certain creed or belonging to a religious organization. I am talking about an intimate, personal relationship with God, made possible by confessing your sinfulness and inviting Jesus Christ to be your personal Savior and the master of your life and marriage.

When a husband and wife are living in a vital relationship with God and trying to express that relationship in practical terms, the marriage is deeply enriched. You bring to your marriage a perspective quite different from the popular "what's in it for me" culture. Marriage counselors agree that the biggest obstacle to overcoming marital troubles is selfishness. When *my way* is more important than *my marriage*, a crack develops in the marital foundation. A vital relationship with God and a deliberate determination to live out biblical principles counteracts our instinctive tendency towards selfishness. Servanthood, sacrifice, trust, and esteeming others better than ourselves are key relational teachings of the Bible. It also speaks of forgiveness, love, affirmation, and flexibility.

> *When my way is more important than my marriage, a crack develops in the marital foundation.*

Your relationship with God also tempers the potentially rash decisions and verbal explosions that threaten great marriages. It keeps you from getting into trouble and provides a way out of trouble. The presence of God's Spirit in your marriage is a powerful resource, helping you to confess your wrongs to each other, to grant forgiveness as required, and to pray together.

The way you relate to God shapes your motivation in building a healthy relationship with your spouse. Gary Thomas' book, *Sacred Marriage*, has greatly encouraged Cindy and me. We have read it separately, studied it together with other couples, passed it on to others, and continued to be challenged by it. In a devotional book based on *Sacred Marriage*, he writes about our spiritual motivation to build a great marriage:

It all comes down to this: Are you a God-centered spouse or a spouse-centered spouse? A spouse-centered spouse acts nicely toward her husband when he acts nicely toward her. She is accommodating, as long as her husband pays her attention. A spouse-centered husband will go out of his way for his wife, as long as she remains agreeable and affectionate. He'll romance her, as long as he feels rewarded for doing so.

A God-centered spouse feels more motivated by his or her commitment to God than by whatever response a spouse may give.[1]

God-centered spouses are more satisfied in their marriages. They consistently rate their marriages as stronger and more satisfying spiritually, emotionally, socially, and sexually. The source of that strength is seen in this verse, "Though one may be overpowered, two can defend themselves. A cord of three strands is not quickly broken" (Ecclesiastes 4:12). You, your spouse, and God form an unbreakable cord. As long as you hear and obey His words, your marriage will be all that He designed it to be.

COMMITMENT TO GOD'S DESIGN FOR MARRIAGE

In the animal kingdom, there are some interesting examples of how different species relate to their mates. The Black Widow spider devours her companion after their ritual mating. Male sea lions build their harems and have been known to injure or kill their families to defend their turf. The female elephant dominates the male and kicks him out of the herd. Then, there are snakes that mate in a casual rendezvous, only to slither off into the dark with no thought of long-term commitment.

God established a different order for the pinnacle of his creation.

These days we act as if marriage is simply a human invention, rather than an institution rooted in creation. In the beginning, God said, "A man will leave his father and mother and be united to his wife, and they will become one flesh" (Genesis 2:24). He created us male and female to walk together, side by side, for a lifetime. By God's design, the love of a man and woman is fulfilled in the wholeness of their life together in the covenant of marriage.

Marriage, as designed by God, begins with a leaving of all other relationships. Perhaps you've heard the saying that the wedding ring is designed to cut-off your circulation. It's not that you and your spouse spend the rest of your lives in solitary confinement. Rather, the bonds to others must be altered in character, so that the man's full commitment is now to his wife and the woman's full commitment is now to her husband. The effect of this principle is that other things and relationships are given a lesser priority – business, career, church ministry, parents, friends, and even children. All these must be placed in proper perspective. Whatever is important to you in this life, aside from a relationship with God, should be less important than your marriage.

Another element in God's design for marriage is that a man and a woman "become one flesh." This is more than simple togetherness. It is the blending of two lives into one – one in mind, heart, body, and spirit. This unity and oneness in marriage is a lifelong process, not an instant fact. Being pronounced husband and wife at the altar makes you one in the legal sense of the word, but what you do in the rest of your married life determines the practical outcome of becoming one. It requires holy wisdom, understanding, and knowledge for completion. It is one man and one woman willingly blending into each other's lives and seeking to glorify God as they do.

Let's do a little experiment. Find two candles and light them. One candle represents the husband and the other represents the wife. As you look at the two flames of your candles, take some time to reflect on the positive characteristics you each bring to your marriage.

Next, move the two candles closer to each other. As you do, think of the ways you have left other human relationships and bonds to blend your lives together. Tip the two candles toward each other and let the flames merge. What do you notice about the changing characteristics of the flames? The flames grow brighter as they merge into one. Look closely. You can still see the individual characteristics of the single flames, but now they have merged those characteristics for the benefit of the one flame. The more you tip the flames toward each other, the more distinct the single flame becomes. You can also see that while letting the candles touch each other at the top, the melting wax begins to create a bond that holds them in place. The two have become one.

God designed marriage for keeps. It involves an unswerving loyalty and a belonging to each other in a permanent union, no matter what.

Becoming one also demands an inseparable joining of one man and one woman throughout their lifetime. In the Hebrew and Greek languages of the Bible, the concept of marital unity comes from words that mean, "to cling to or adhere to; to be joined together." There is a sense of permanence in the relationship. Jesus recognized this in his earthly ministry. When answering a question about marriage and divorce, he decreed that "what God has joined together, let man not separate" (Matthew 19:6). God designed marriage for keeps. It involves an unswerving loyalty and a belonging to each other in a permanent union, no matter what.

Once on a hot, hazy, and humid summer day, I walked to the Post Office to buy some stamps. Placing them in my shirt pocket, I continued through my daily routine. Arriving home at the end of the day, I discovered that the two layers of stamps in the booklet had stuck together. This was back in the days when postage stamps required you to moisten the glue on them before applying them to the envelope – the old lick and stick method.

Since they were apparently useless to me, I returned them to the Post Office, requesting an exchange, only to discover that "all sales are final." How was I to use them? The clerk obviously had confronted this dilemma with other customers. He peeled back one corner of the bonded strips, then swiftly separated the two layers of stamps. Handing the book of stamps back to me, he wished me a good day. "Are they still usable?" I asked. "Of course," he said.

Unity and oneness in marriage is not automatic. It is the result of discipline, determination, and hard work.

I have long remembered that day, as I reflected on the similarity between what God says about marriage, and the bonding of those stamps. You see, those two layers of stamps had become one. They were bonded in much the same way God has designed the marriage relationship. What I saw after the tearing apart of the two layers reminded me that divorce leaves its mark on all involved. When the two layers were pulled apart, ink spots from the printed side of the second layer stayed on the sticky underside of the top layer. I realized that as those stamps traveled along wherever we sent the envelopes, they carried the impact and imprint of that bonding experience.

Such is the power of the bond that takes place in marriage. We are no longer two, but one. Tear us apart and we carry the influence of that bonding experience into future relationships.

Unity and oneness in marriage is not automatic. It is the result of discipline, determination, and hard work. It's an inflexible commitment to a marriage that honors God's presence in your lives and one that you want your children to duplicate. By following God's design for marriage, you can build a marriage that will survive and thrive in the midst of life's challenges.

THE POWER OF PRAYER

Do not underestimate the power of prayer in your marriage. It is by prayer that we enlist the influence of God in our lives. We ask him to do what we cannot do. When a couple prays, it has several effects.

It helps you with your perspective on problems, and clears your vision so you can see what God wants in the foggy, murky moments of your lives. Your heart is quieted. You cannot worry and pray at the same time. The Bible says, "Do not be anxious about anything, but in everything, by prayer and petition, with thanksgiving, present your requests to God. And the peace of God, which transcends all understanding, will guard your hearts and your minds in Christ Jesus" (Philippians 4:6-7). Through sincere prayer, you can gain God's perspective on an issue, which often helps you discover the solution to your dilemma.

Prayer helps you reorder your priorities. It activates your faith in God, puts him and his plan first in your lives, and forces you to leave the situation with him. Through prayer, you can also find that what you highly value may be a deterrent to God's blessings in your home.

Prayer gives you a sense of purpose. Through contact with God, you discover how he wants to use your marriage for his glory. Your prayers reduce your daily cares and keep you in a place where God can use you most effectively.

How do you make prayer a significant part of your marriage? First, agree together that you will make this a priority in your marriage. The biggest reason couples give for not praying is the lack of time. The truth is that we make time for what we want. Find a mutually agreeable time to pray together. You may have to get up a few minutes before the kids so you can have some privacy, or turn off the TV earlier in the evening so you can pray before you go to bed.

Keep the prayer time brief. It is not necessary to pray for hours as a couple in order to have a meaningful prayer life. If one of you is not comfortable praying aloud, the shorter time will be encouraging. You can always extend the time when that is mutually agreeable.

How you pray together is up to you, but taking turns praying short prayers back and forth in a conversational style helps you stay focused. Don't go on and on. Give your spouse a chance. When one spouse has nothing more to say, simply say, "Amen."

Do not forget to pray for your marriage. Now, be careful when you pray for your spouse in the presence of him or her. Praying about the way in which your spouse needs to change, or about some sin in his or her life, is not effective or loving; unless, he or she asked you to pray about those things. Your spouse is not likely to respond well to that style. It is better to give thanks to God for your spouse, for the good things in him or her, and for the fact that God brought you together.

In our marriage seminars, I distribute a card that contains several model prayers for married couples written by Riette Woods.[2] Each prayer, grounded in Scripture, helps couples focus on key qualities of a great marriage. Here are three examples:

- *Unity – Knit our hearts together in complete unity. Teach us how to address things that hinder our relationship, and help us work through our differences with compassion and gentleness. Enable us to rejoice in and encourage each other's strengths and gifts, and empower us through Your Spirit to overcome individual weak-nesses and sins. (Ephesians 5:31; Colossians 3:12; 1 Corinthians 12:4-27; Galatians 5:16)*

- *Physical Intimacy – Kindle the passion between us, God. Give us a hunger for each other, and let us be sa-tisfied with one another. Keep our union pure and holy in every way. (Song of Solomon 7:10; Proverbs 5:15-19; Hebrews 13:4; 1 Peter 1:15-16)*

- *Protection – Lord Jesus, You desire our marriage to last a lifetime. Protect, preserve, and sustain it. Do not allow sin, the enemy, circumstances, difficulties, or other people to separate what you have joined together. (Malachi 2:13-16; Matthew 19:3-9)*

I like using Scripture to guide me in praying for others. The Apostle Paul's prayer for the Ephesians serves as a model for how I pray for Cindy:

I pray that out of his glorious riches he may strengthen you with power through his Spirit in your inner being, so that Christ may dwell in your hearts through faith. And I pray that you, being rooted and established in love, may have power, together with all the saints, to grasp how wide and long and high and deep is the love of Christ, and to know this love that surpasses knowledge – that you may be filled to the measure of all the fullness of God. – Ephesians 3:16-19

AN AUTHENTIC CHRISTIAN LIFESTYLE

A house foundation appears strong on the outside, even if it doesn't have enough steel rebar reinforcing the concrete. However, the weight of the house and its contents, coupled with changes in the earth's surface, will reveal its weakness and its lack of authenticity. "Authentic" describes something that is shown to be trustworthy, true, and reliable. Consistency would be another way of saying it. An authentic person lives a life that matches his or her values and priorities.

A couple building a marriage that glorifies God will not tolerate inconsistency between their core faith values (or beliefs) and their actions in marriage. For example, Cindy and I believe strongly that we should worship together with other believers. That means we do not debate whether we go to church. Of course, I was a local church pastor for many years, which meant I had to be there. However, even when we are on vacation we do not avoid gathering with other Christians to worship God and learn from the Bible. The practicing of this core spiritual value helps bond us as a couple and strengthens us for any stormy weather in our marriage.

To know what is right and not do it, tears at the fibers of your integrity. It weakens the soul of your marriage.

Committing to an authentic Christian lifestyle has also helped us make other decisions, such as what kind of TV shows and movies we watch, where our money goes, issues related to addictive behaviors, and how we treat each other. To know what is right and not do it, tears at the fibers of your integrity. It weakens the soul of your marriage. Remember, the spiritual character of your marriage is the result of how you live what you believe.

SPIRITUAL TOGETHERNESS

Often spiritual beliefs are practiced individually and not integrated into the couple relationship. Although some people regard faith in God as a private matter, a shared spiritual intimacy does strengthen a marriage. Cultivating your spiritual togetherness is a critical part of a great marital foundation. Dr. Charles Sell, a marriage and family ministry educator, wrote the following about this topic:

> *Whenever anyone asks me what is the one most important facet of a Christian marriage, I answer quickly: spiritual oneness. If building a marriage were compared to baking a loaf of bread, the one ingredient that would compare to yeast would be the spiritual togetherness. More than anything, how you relate to God may determine whether or not your marriage rises successfully or falls disappointingly flat.[3]*

Spiritual togetherness will not make your marriage perfect; however, it will keep you in touch with the One who has the answers to your deepest marriage problems.

What can you do to further enhance your spiritual togetherness? Here are some suggestions:

- Read the Bible or a devotional book together.

- Talk together about what God is teaching you in your personal devotions and studies.

- Pray together aloud or silently. Holding hands during this time is a blessing.

- Attend a Bible study with other married couples.

- Make your devotions simple and brief.

- Make Sundays relaxed. Replace the race to church with relaxation and heart preparation.

- Be accountable to each other; sharing and receiving correction from each other.

- Compliment your spouse on his or her spiritual growth (no matter how small it might be).

- Spend time with other Christian couples who share your core spiritual values.

- Together seek God's will for your life and marriage.

- Count the blessings of God in your life and marriage. We call them, "God-sightings."

- Encourage the expression of spiritual gifts in ministry as a couple. You may have different interests, but if you can find a place where you can minister as a team, you will strengthen your spiritual togetherness.

Time pressures and the daily distractions of life can erode your commitment to a strong spiritual foundation. Resist! The spiritual bonds of your marriage are the most intimate aspects of your relationship. Building a great marriage on a great foundation requires a lot of effort and energy, but isn't your marriage worth it?

 TOOL TIME FOR COUPLES

1. List three things you and your spouse do that promote unity and oneness in your marriage. What more could you do?

2. Discuss with your spouse how you would answer if someone were to ask you, "In what ways is your marriage uniquely Christian?"

3. After reading this chapter, what are three things you and your spouse want to do in the next 30 days to strengthen the spiritual foundation of your marriage? How and when will you do it?

CHAPTER 3

Becoming a Host in Your Marriage

On a rerun of the "Seinfeld" television show, Jerry and a girlfriend pretend to be married in order to get a discount on dry cleaning. Afterwards, in the coffee shop, they toast each other with orange juice.

"To my beautiful wife."

"To my adoring husband."

"Adoring? What about handsome?"

"I like adoring."

"Adoring's good for you, but what does it do for me?"[1]

That's the question you ask when your marriage is all about you. It's no wonder so many people today bail out of their marriages. They are only interested in what it is doing for them.

"What does it do for me?" is burned into your human nature. As a little child, your parents took care of you and provided for your care and nurture. You didn't have to do much. As you got older, your parents gave your more responsibilities, but they were still responsible for providing you with the basic needs of food, shelter, clothing, and education. Moving into single adulthood, you learned to take care of yourself. Then, you were married and discovered you had to put someone else first. That can take some adjusting.

Cecil Osborne wrote in *Understanding Your Mate*, "There are many reasons for the breakup of marriages, but the most common one is never found in divorce complaints: both of the marriage partners are waiting for each other to meet their needs."[2] A vital tool in building a great marriage is mutual servanthood, or becoming a host. It's one of the fundamental things that makes a marriage work and last for a lifetime. When you are a guest, everything is done for you. You feel no sense of responsibility or initiative. It's nice to be a guest, to be entertained and pampered, just to relax, indulge, and enjoy. However, if each marriage partner is hoping to be a guest, expecting the other to exercise initiative for his or her benefit, there will be big trouble. Both will be disappointed. The marriage becomes stale, loses its attractiveness, and an affair becomes tempting.

In a great marriage, each spouse focuses on becoming a host, not a guest in the relationship. In doing so, we are following the example of Jesus, who said:

> *...whoever wants to become great among you must be your servant, and whoever wants to be first must be slave of all. For even the Son of Man did not come to be served, but to serve, and give his life as a ransom for many. – Mark 10:43-45*

Servanthood is essential for greatness. Even the Son of God did not consider servanthood beneath his calling. Jesus did not sit around waiting for his disciples to serve him. His mission and life on earth focused on others as he fed the multitudes, healed the sick, and raised the dead. In addition, he came to earth to meet our greatest need – salvation from the consequences of sin.

SELFISHNESS: THE ENEMY OF A GREAT MARRIAGE

No marriage can accommodate selfish people who think only about themselves. Selfishness drives people apart, leaving no room for compromise and teamwork. A strong, satisfying marriage must have two hosts – each personally committed to the active initiative role of the mature adult, not the passive receptive role of the spoiled child. I read about a wedding where the groom, instead of going through the traditional garter ceremony, brought out a basin of water and washed his bride's feet. The wedding guests probably thought he was crazy, but he had it right. Most people do not enter marriage thinking about becoming a servant.

Mutual service is a power tool in great marriages because God intended your union to be a partnership, with each of you equally responsible for the marriage's well being. Becoming a host in your marriage means, without expecting something in return, you persistently watch for ways to love, assist, support, praise, appreciate, protect, and please your spouse. Jim Mueller, the founder of *Growthtrac*, made the following confession on how he misunderstood servanthood in his marriage:

> *Before I truly understood what it meant to serve Sheri, I would perform acts of kindness expecting something in return. For example, if I washed Sheri's car, I expected her to bake me chocolate chip cookies. Or if I went grocery*

45

shopping, I counted on a romantic encounter later that night. Even though my expectations were left unstated, there was an underlying hope that Sheri would recipro-cate.[3]

A complaint heard often in a distressed marriage is, "My spouse doesn't respect me or my needs." Marriage can be demanding and frustrating. At times, you may find yourself not being courteous to each other. You stop seeing your spouse as important, and begin putting other things – work, hobbies or the children – before the marriage.

However, couples in great marriages make the needs of their spouse a priority and make an effort not to take each other for granted. They follow the counsel of the Apostle Paul, "Do nothing from selfish ambition or vain conceit, but in humility consider others better than yourselves. Each of you should look not only to your own interests, but also to the interests of others" (Philippians 2:3-4).

Desperate households are filled with competing egos, but households devoted to God work to cultivate a servant heart in their relationships.

What happens to your spouse when you think only about yourself? It's as if you were standing on his or her air hose. Just as we need air to breathe, we all have certain emotional needs we want met in marriage. If you step on your spouse's air hose for any length of time, cutting off the oxygen supply, you can expect him or her to start thrashing around to get that need met. He or she could even step on your air hose to see if you will get the message. The same thing happens when needs are not met in marriage. A spouse, who longs for love, attention, respect, and acceptance, may lash out with negative attacks that create more distance in the marriage. On the other hand, they may take a passive-aggressive approach, "I won't meet any of your needs until you meet my needs."

God values a spirit of humility and servanthood, and expects us to display this attribute in our marriages. Desperate households are filled with competing egos, but households devoted to God work to cultivate a servant heart in their relationships. A marriage characterized by prideful attitudes is destined for trouble. Blaise Pascal, a 17th century philosopher and theologian, declared, "The virtue of a man ought to be measured, not by his extraordinary exertions, but by his everyday conduct." How true! The way you daily serve as a host in your marriage reveals the heart you have for your spouse.

HIS NEEDS – HER NEEDS – OUR NEEDS

We are not expected to meet every need of our spouse. That would be unwise, exhausting, and impossible. However, four fundamental needs are basic to building a great marriage.

The Need for Attention – Each of us wants to be noticed for who we are and for what we do. Bad marriages always include self-centered people. It's all about them. One hurting wife said this about her husband, "He never notices my cooking, the way I look, or how I try to keep the house for him. He never pays attention to me. He takes me for granted and I really don't think I'm important to him." A husband who looked for attention outside of his marriage said, "I had come to feel like no more than a piece of furniture. I was nobody around my own home, nobody worth noticing, listening to, or loving. I got fed up. Not long ago I walked right out the door."

Mature people, who think beyond themselves, build great marriages. Instead of seeing marriage as a place to get attention, mature people make it a place where attention is given generously. It's not what you want or how you are doing. It's more about a focus on your spouse:

- Notice her new haircut or new outfit.

- Be interested in watching the game with him.

- Ask what you can do to help her with the kids.

- Give him twenty minutes of your undivided attention to find out what his day was like.

The Need for Acceptance – A genuine desire to serve my wife encourages me to satisfy her need for acceptance. Accepting her unconditionally tells her I have an awareness of her unique value as my wife.

> *Demanding that your spouse match your fantasies is an insult. It breeds division, resentment, and anger.*

Early in our marriage, I wanted Cindy to sing duets in church with me, but she was not comfortable being in the spotlight. After attempting to coerce her to fulfill my fantasy, it became clear that I was communicating a rejection of her unique personhood. She told me that she bet I wished I had married someone else.

God used that exchange to get my attention. Her gifts and abilities are more suited for other ministry areas. Trying to remake her was an effort to meet my need, not hers.

Demanding that your spouse match your fantasies is an insult. It breeds division, resentment, and anger. Unconditional acceptance of your mate's individual value is so important. If you accept only in part, you can love only in part.

Acceptance does not necessarily mean approval. It does mean accepting reality as it is. It recognizes what cannot be changed, as well as what can be changed. In a great marriage, acceptance is willing to live with the differences.

The Need for Affection – A host in a great marriage will also seek to meet his or her spouse's need for affection. The things that sparked the passion in the days of courtship and early marriage – touching, holding hands, hugging, and kissing – cannot be stashed away in the closet with all of the old wedding announcements. You don't build a great marriage with the attitude of the guy who asked, "Why do you have to keep chasing the bus once you've caught it?"

John and Emilia Rocchio had been married for 83 years when I first read about them. At the time, they had the distinction of being one of the longest married couples in the world. They began marriage with more dreams than dollars. Their pastor was not convinced that their marriage would last. It did, and everyone wanted to know the secret to their success. Here are their answers:

> *"Secret? What secret?" John said. "I live a normal life. She feeds me good."*
>
> *"And he never criticized me," Emilia added. "He liked everything I did."*
>
> *Just as important, both have always shown affection for each other. "We've always held hands," John says. "My mother would ask Emilia, 'Hey, are you afraid he's going to run away? We don't hold hands in Italy.' And Emilia would say, 'We do hold hands here in America.'"*[i]

That is 83 years of affection. To meet your spouse's need for

TOOLS FOR A GREAT MARRIAGE

affection, Dr. Randy Carlson, a family therapist, recommends that you learn his or her affection language. Using the list below, try to figure out which one is your spouse's primary way of showing affection, and then, let your spouse know which one is yours:

- *A hand person – One who appreciates practical ways of showing affection, such as working together on a shared project.*

- *A heart person – One who appreciates ways of connecting emotionally, such as through speaking affirming words.*

- *A head person – One who enjoys sharing intellectual pursuits with you, such as reading or taking a class together.* [5]

Now that you know your spouse's affection language, you can be intentional about meeting this need. Couples wanting to have a great marriage will work together to express affection in ways they each genuinely appreciate. Here are some more suggestions you can practice daily in your marriage:

- Hug and kiss your spouse when you first get up in the morning (after using a breath freshener!).

- Tell your spouse you love her or him each morning.

- Call your spouse during the day to ask how he or she is doing and say that you love him or her.

- When you arrive home from work, spend a few

minutes talking to your spouse about how his or
her day went.

- Help your spouse with the housework and the
  children.

- Hug and kiss in bed before you both go to sleep.

The Need for Admiration – Your spouse also has a need for admiration.
Most people's emotional stability is enhanced or diminished by what
others think and say about them. One husband said, "Marriage invests
each moment and action with significance.
Everything I do and say matters to someone
else – my wife." Some of us go months and
even years without giving a personal word of
admiration to our spouse, and wonder why the
relationship seems to be in a rut. When you
affirm your spouse with loving words and
deeds, your spouse is more likely to love you
deeper.

> *Couples who
> nurture their
> fondness and
> admiration for
> one another are
> better able to
> accept each
> other's flaws and
> prevent them
> from threatening
> their marriages.*

     Before marriage, it's easy to see the posi-
tive attributes and ignore the things that bug
you. As the years pass, or in some cases
months, the stars in your eyes begin to fade
and you find it easy to zero in on your spouse's
annoying quirks. The reality of living together does create tension and
before you know what is happening, you see only the things you don't
like.

     Marital researcher, John Gottman, has found that people, who are
happily married, like each other. That may seem obvious, but it needs
to be emphasized. Couples who nurture their fondness and admiration

for one another are better able to accept each other's flaws, and prevent them from threatening their marriages. Genuine admiration for your spouse protects you against feeling contempt, which can quickly break down the bonds of friendship between husband and wife.

To build a great marriage on a daily basis, actively look for the positive. Concentrate on your spouse's strengths. You already know the weak areas, so look for strengths. Give honest compliments. Fight the urge to point out his or her shortcomings and focus on what you appreciate about your spouse. You may be pleasantly surprised by his or her response.

THE CHALLENGE TO BECOMING A HOST

A challenge to mutual servanthood in your marriage is whether you are willing to let your spouse serve you. Are you willing to let your spouse into your life, to let him or her know how best to serve you? This requires vulnerability and humility. Gary Thomas writes in *Sacred Marriage*, "Service includes allowing your spouse to give – if, of course they are willing to give. In other words, service isn't just washing somebody else's feet; at times it's letting *your own* feet be washed."[6] Don't let your pride get in the way of your spouse becoming a host in your marriage.

A second challenge to marital servanthood is the *pleaseability* factor. Do you appreciate what your spouse does to serve you, or are you someone who is never satisfied? In a great marriage, a spouse declares his or her thanksgiving for the servanthood efforts of the other spouse. There is joy in serving a spouse who is pleased by what you do. Author and pastor, Gordon MacDonald, tells how he learned about the style of *unpleaseability* from a bird book:

> *The male house wren is a habitual nest starter. He stuffs*

any likely nesting cavity with twigs, grass, and other materials perhaps to mark his territory and perhaps as an inducement to the females when they arrive. As soon as they appear, the busy male sings to draw their attention. He courts one ardently, wings quivering, tail flickering straight up. If she proves receptive, he escorts her around his prospective nest sites. The female almost always disapproves of her mate's homebuilding efforts. After she selects one of his sites, she usually removes all the materials and starts the nest all over again. Sometimes she collects strange items. One nest contained 52 hairpins, 188 nails, 4 tacks, 13 staples, 10 pins, 11 safety pins, 6 paperclips, 2 hooks, 3 garter fasteners, and a buckle. Talk about hard to please. One can see the forlorn shake of the male's head, after all his hard work, as he sees his new wife completely tear apart his creative efforts. I suspect that one could also imagine his irritation every time he steps on one of the tacks.[7]

A third challenge in becoming a host in your marriage is when you do not feel like it, due to deep hurt and resentment. If you go for long periods without attention, acceptance, affection, or admiration, you can easily become vulnerable to moodiness, retaliation, or rejection. It may not always be convenient or easy to reach out to your spouse. The challenge is to show your love by serving, even when you don't feel like it. As you choose to love in this way, the feelings will come and your spouse is more likely to respond in the same manner.

I heard Dr. Gary Chapman, author of *The Five Love Languages*, tell about the way he learned to make the principle of servanthood practical in his marriage. As he struggled through a difficult time, he discovered that he lacked an attitude of servanthood. As he puts it, "I had made demands of my wife. I had expected her to make me happy." His marriage began to change when he asked Karolyn these questions:

- *How can I help you?*

- *How can I make your life easier?*

- *How can I be a better husband to you?*

Their marriage changed when he let her teach him how he could serve her. It did not happen overnight, because the pain had been there too long, but change did occur.[8]

What will happen if your spouse is not actively serving in a host role in your marriage? Your first reaction may be to do the same thing. Surely, that will get his or her attention, you reason. There is no guarantee of that. Your second reaction may be to look outside your marriage. While others can meet these needs, be careful of emotional attachments that may develop with someone of the opposite sex. Adulterous affairs do not always begin with a physical, sexual attraction. Instead, they begin when someone touches an emotional vacuum that is not filled in the marriage. Emotional affairs are very real and damaging to the covenant of marriage.

> *Emotional affairs are very real and damaging to the covenant of marriage.*

Instead of focusing on what you are missing, consider being proactive in loving your spouse. Take a step back for a moment and examine your marriage. Forget what you need, or want, and focus on the expressed needs of your husband or wife. Make an honest assessment as to whether you are doing everything, within reason, to meet those needs. While you may be in need of emotional refreshing, consider this wise observation, "Those who refresh others will themselves be refreshed" (Proverbs 11:25). You must learn to surrender your doubts and insecurities, and take a big step outside of your comfort zone. As you serve your spouse in a humble and gentle way, you will find refreshment in doing the right thing.

 TOOL TIME FOR COUPLES

1. When you got married, which expectation was dominant?

   - I will meet my spouse's needs.

   - My spouse will meet my needs.

2. How has this aided or interfered with your ability to approach marriage with a servant's heart?

3. Discuss with your spouse the ways in which he or she could meet the needs listed below in your life.

   - Need for Attention

   - Need for Acceptance

   - Need for Affection

   - Need for Admiration

4. What do you think would be the greatest improvement in your marriage if you and your spouse became better servants of one another? What is the most significant change you would have to make to see this happen?

CHAPTER 4

What's Love Got
to Do With It?

What's love got to do with a great marriage? Without love, there would be no wedding and no marriage. Love is so important to the marriage relationship that we would sacrifice prime rib for it. At least that is the implication of this proverb, "Better a meal of vegetables where there is love than a fattened calf with hatred" (Proverbs 15:17).

Most of us begin our relationships with a kind of love that has been described as a feeling you feel when you get a feeling you never felt before. It's an exhilarating time. We are obsessed with each other. We believe that as long as those feelings are present, the marriage will last forever, the love will not fade. Nothing could ever come between us. Other couples will have troubles, but not us. Our love will hold us together.

However, that love is lived out in the pressure-cooker days of our lives. On top of building a great marriage, there are career demands, kids to raise, and perhaps aging parents to care for in their golden years. Marriages have been blown apart by unfulfilled and unrealistic expectations, unfortunate circumstances, and unwise choices. Somehow, the love these couples had was not strong enough. This letter from a young wife captures the pain and despair when the love feelings are lost:

> *We have been having many problems and just recently, it has gotten worse. I wish I had done things differently because I'm not sure we are going to make it. My heart is breaking into a million pieces and I don't know if there is anything I can do. He says he doesn't love me anymore and I don't know how to fix that.*

Love is very important in building great marriages, but the kind of love that exists in a great marriage is more than a feeling.

WHAT IS LOVE?

When asked to describe *love*, a group of children gave answers that describe the kind of love found in a great marriage:

- *When my grandmother got arthritis, she couldn't bend over and paint her toenails anymore. So my grandfather does it for her all the time, even when his hands got arthritis too. That's love.*

- *When someone loves you, the way they say your name is different. You know that your name is safe in their mouth.*

- *Love is when my mommy makes coffee for my daddy*

and she takes a sip before giving it to him, to make sure the taste is OK.

- *Love is when you kiss all the time. Then when you get tired of kissing, you still want to be together and you talk more. My mommy and Daddy are like that. They look gross when they kiss.*

- *Love is like a little old woman and a little old man who are still friends even after they know each other so well.*

- *Love is when mommy gives daddy the best piece of chicken.*

These answers reflect a love rooted in a choice of the will, not just emotions. I'm not against feelings. But what holds a marriage together when the feelings of love are sparse?

Dr. Robert Sternberg, a professor at Yale University, did extensive research to answer the question, "What is love?" As a result, he developed his *Triangular Theory of Love*,[1] which does a good job of describing the ingredients of marital love. Sternberg says that love consists of the following three components:

- *Passion* – This is the physical attraction, sexual desire, and strong emotional attraction you have to another person. Without the other two ingredients of love, this infatuated love may disappear quickly.

- *Intimacy* – This is the closeness and connectedness of marriage. It is friendship, where you understand and accept each other, which fosters open and intimate communication in your marriage.

- *Commitment* – This is a matter of the will, where you consciously decide that you love someone and you commit to maintain that love.

While Sternberg's research is informative, he did not find anything new. You probably recognize how Sternberg's components parallel the Greek words that are often translated as love:

- Passion = *Eros*

- Intimacy/Friendship = *Phileo*

- Commitment = *Agape*

Sternberg says that when all three ingredients of love – passion, intimacy, and commitment – strongly exist in your marriage, you have a *consummate love* for your spouse, for which we all strive in our marriages. Maintaining this consummate love may be even harder than achieving it.

AN ENDURING LOVE

Eventually, every good marriage hits a rough patch. In your marriage vows, you promised to love regardless of all the changes and adversities, regardless of the good times or the bad times, and regardless of whether you live in wealth or poverty. I heard someone comment that instead of going into a marriage vowing, "till death do us part," maybe brides and grooms should be asked, "Do you have any idea how difficult this is going to be?"

A great marriage embodies a love of commitment, endurance, and perseverance. Not particularly romantic, is it? However, a relationship solely based on romance and emotions has an average life span of about two years.[2] You have to have something more to make it last a lifetime.

The something more is an *enduring love*, which is the ability to stick with the relationship through the changing seasons of life – "for better or for worse, for richer or for poorer, in sickness and in health, to love and to cherish till death do us part." The Apostle Paul described this enduring love in the famous "love chapter" of the Bible:

> *Love is patient and kind. Love is not jealous or boastful or proud or rude. Love does not demand its own way. Love is not irritable, and it keeps no record of when it has been wronged. It is never glad about injustice but rejoices whenever the truth wins out. Love never gives up, never loses faith, is always hopeful, and endures through every circumstance.* – 1 Corinthians 13:4-7, NLT

When you look closely at these verses, you can learn several things about this holy kind of love:

- *It is an active love – something you do.* You are patient when his dirty clothes continually miss the clothes hamper. You are kind when she borrows your tools, but forgets to put them back in the toolbox.

- *It is premeditated.* You decide ahead of time to respond in a loving manner when you are proven wrong in the middle of an intense argument.

- *It is observable.* You can see it in action. It's not just an emotion that is deep within your soul, only known to you. Other people see whether you are rude to each other, whether you are selfish and demanding, and whether you hold grudges.

- *It is measurable and verifiable.* You can quantify it. Elizabeth Barrett Browning, an English poet wrote, "How do I love thee? Let me count the ways."[3] Her answer was a list of the ways she measured that love, the depth, the height, and the breadth of it. Dr. Gary Chapman, author of *The Five Love Languages*, says that we all have an emotional love tank waiting to be filled and that we can measure its content. Ask your spouse this question, "On a scale of 0-10, how full is your love tank?" The answer may surprise you. Then, ask him or her to tell you one thing you could do to raise that number a couple of points.

An enduring love chooses to keep on loving when loving your spouse is not particularly satisfying. It's easy to love someone who is good to you, shows kindness daily, and responds to your loving words or actions with the same love. We love them *because* of what they do. Gary Thomas confronts this style of loving with this challenge:

> *Will you love only "because"? Or are you willing to love "anyway"? Will you love a man or woman who doesn't appreciate your sacrifice on his or her behalf? Will you love a husband or wife who takes you for granted? Will you love a spouse who isn't nearly as kind to you as you are to him or her?*
>
> *Almost every faithless marriage is based on "because" love. Christians are called to "anyway" love. That's what makes us different.*[4]

What a refreshing concept in our self-centered culture! When we love each other *anyway*, we are modeling God's love, an enduring love, in our marriages. He loves us even when we ignore him and take for granted his boundless grace and mercy. He doesn't like it, but he continues to love us. To love *anyway* is to love like God. You keep reaching out to honor your spouse, trusting God to provide for your own needs.

KEEPING LOVE ALIVE

George and Rita remembered two significant moments in their marriage. The first happened when they looked at each other near the beginning of their relationship with the full knowledge of loving and being loved. They felt fully alive. Fifteen years later, they stood before each other and suddenly saw a stranger. Their relationship and attitudes had been shaped by too many hurts and unresolved anger. Fighting had become the norm, rather than the exception in their marriage. Emotionally drained from all of the struggles, they were considering a trial separation. No longer was their love fully alive.

Was there anything George and Rita could have done to avoid their situation? Are there practical steps you can take to avoid landing in the same place? If you are where they were, can you rekindle the flame that once burned between you? My answer is a resounding, "Yes!" Here are three things you can do to keep love alive in your marriage:

Do Not Forget to be Married. – Seven-time Tour de France winner, Lance Armstrong, was quite candid about his marriage in the book, *Every Second Counts.* He knows about discipline, determination, and hard work. Not only has he excelled at bike racing, but he did so while battling cancer. Yet, he tells of his regret that he did not put the same hard work into his marriage. He says, "All I knew was that in trying to do everything, we'd forgotten to do the most important thing. We forgot to be married."[5]

Couples let many things intrude on their marriage relationship – careers, hobbies, friends, and even children. So much energy is put into these other roles; there is nothing left for their relationship. In time, they stop playing, laughing, touching, and communicating with each other. The sad thing is that these couples settle for a functional relationship, putting aside the romance, passion, and intimacy of marriage. They may live under the same roof and sleep in the same bed, but their marriage is lost in the myriad duties and demands of daily life.

> *To keep love alive in your marriage, you must give top priority to maintaining a loving relationship with your spouse.*

To keep love alive in your marriage, you must give top priority to maintaining a loving relationship with your spouse. If your work or even your children have become the primary focus of your life, you need to refocus on your spouse, rather than looking to another individual or group of people to meet your emotional needs. Each area of your life must be put into proper perspective. Whatever is important to you in this life, other than your relationship with God, should be less important than your marriage. There is much to enjoy and do in this life, but don't forget to be married.

Cherish and Respect Your Spouse as Your Best Friend. – At its root, marriage is not just sex, romance, emotional highs, or pleasure. The core of marriage is a friendship built on emotional closeness, acceptance of one another, and a fulfilling companionship. In survey after survey, the overwhelming majority of couples in successful long-term marriages reported that they had become best friends. This was evident in our marriage on one particular wedding anniversary. Cindy gave me a card with the following statement: "It's one thing to be in love. It's another to be good friends. And it's a wonderful thing to be madly in love with my best friend!" I still have the card displayed in my study.

Best friends practice several key habits. They stay in touch with each other as they share themselves and their experiences, support each other during troubled times, and consistently affirm one another. They also have discovered the extreme value of mutually respecting each other.

One of the ways I show respect to my wife is to regard her as the precious personal property of the King of kings and Lord of lords. The Apostle Paul writes, "Do you not know that your body is the temple of the Holy Spirit, who is in you, whom you have received from God? You are not your own; you were bought at a price" (Romans 6:19). This reminds me that God, who gave his only Son to die on the cross for her sins, has purchased Cindy. He loves her as a person of worth and value. Therefore, I am moved to look for ways of acknowledging the worth and value of her life, deeds, thoughts, and opinions.

It's one thing to be in love. It's another to be good friends. And it's a wonderful thing to be madly in love with my best friend!

Love and respect in marriage is not an option for the Christian couple. It is a command of Scripture, without any exemption, as seen here, "However, each one of you must love his wife as he loves himself, and the wife must respect her husband" (Ephesians 5:33). To honor and respect your spouse is not based on whether or not he or she has earned it. It is based on the fact that God considers your spouse worthy of Jesus' sacrificial death on the cross. Even if your spouse is not a Christian, he or she deserves your respect and love because God values them.

Men report that they are motivated and encouraged in their marriages when they feel respected by their wives. When his wife does not respect him, a husband gradually becomes passive and less energized. With each passing day, he has less desire to actively engage his wife in the relationship. On the other hand, when he feels respected and trusted, he will do his best to fulfill his wife's needs. When he feels appreciated for his efforts – even when they fall short of her expectations – he is empowered and will give more of himself to his wife and their marriage.

Women report that in marriage, they are motivated and encouraged when they feel cherished. When a woman does not feel cherished and honored by her husband, she is convinced he does not love her. There is a big hole in her heart. As Dr. Emerson Eggerichs observes, "She will spend her energy seeking to help change him by her loving criticism and complaints, which eventually feel like contempt to him."[6] On the other hand, when she feels loved and cherished by her husband, she is fulfilled and has more to give to their marriage.

Couples who do not cherish and respect each other often end up feeling misunderstood, unappreciated, exploited, and emotionally dead. Another observation by Dr. Eggerichs is that we often focus on our own needs in marriage and overlook the needs of our spouse. He explains that "the wife needs love; she is not trying to be disrespectful. The husband needs respect; he is not trying to be unloving."[7]

Lack of respect and love is evident in the following signs of a dying friendship:

- *Busyness* – You neglect each other because of family schedules, church or community obligations, and careers.

- *Avoidance* – You fail to confront little problems, nega-tive attitudes, and relational ruts until they have grown so large they are quenching your love and respect for each other.

- *Forgetfulness* – You disregard the small bonding beha-viors that help your love grow and remain exciting, such as flowers or candy on a special occasion, breakfast in bed, doing the laundry, and being nice when the other person is irritable.

- *Nit-picking* – You fail to overlook the unimportant flaws, unintentional slights, and minor slip-ups that oc-cur in all friendships.

Does this list hit too close to home in your marriage? If so, the first step in cherishing and respecting your spouse as your best friend is to reverse these destructive actions in your marriage. The next step is to boldly go where few are willing to go. Apologize to your spouse and ask for his or her forgiveness. As you both take responsibility for how you treat each other, you will protect the love in your marriage.

Develop Rituals for Fun. – Keeping love alive in a great marriage does not mean you must focus exclusively on problems nor have an emo-tionally deep and intimate discussion. Spending time having fun together, on a regular basis, is a powerful deterrent to a stale marriage.

Jim and Diane came to see me at a time when the pressures of their careers and family life had them stuck in a negative cycle in their marriage. They loved each other, but did not like each other very much. In the course of our conversation, I asked what they did for fun. When was the last time they went out on a date? I could tell from the way they looked at each other that it had been a long time. Therefore, we spent the next 30 minutes planning a fun date for them. It did not involve a lot of money. I asked them what they enjoyed doing together before they became so busy. They left my office with a plan for fun.

Things were different the next time I saw them. Their body language communicated that they were in a different place in their relationship. They even sat closer to each other. As they talked about their date, it was clear to me they had rediscovered what they liked about being married – they were friends.

> *Couples in great marriages can enjoy good times spent together, knowing they are deeply accepted and that they will be there for one another when tough times come.*

Couples in great marriages can enjoy good times spent together, knowing they are deeply accepted and that they will be there for one another when tough times come. As married life becomes busier, humor often fades, and no time remains for fun. Stressed and tired, couples feel overwhelmed with responsibilities. They forget how to relax and enjoy lighthearted times together. Consumed with routine life events, too many couples spend much of their "quality time" in front of the TV while eating dinner and reading the mail.

Fun is a powerful tool in relieving stress. Make sure you plan regular time alone as a couple for fun. David and Claudia Arp, award-winning authors and international marriage educators, taught us that the main ingredients of a date are privacy, enjoyment, and conversation. Privacy means no group dating or bringing along the children! It can be a nice quiet dinner at a restaurant or a walk along the beach. It doesn't have to cost a lot of money and it should be something both of you can enjoy. Here are some fun dating ideas to spice up your marriage:[8]

- Spend an afternoon at a theatrical production or an opera. They are not as expensive as you might think. Check out a local college for possible discounts on campus performances.

- Sample a variety of cafés, delis, and coffee shops. Instead of just staying at one restaurant, have dinner at one place and dessert at another. Try to find places within walking distance; this way you can enjoy the scenery.

- Head to the zoo. Check out everything from penguins to gorillas. If you are more of an aquatic fan, check out your nearest aquarium.

- Hit the outdoors. Pack a lunch and head to the nearest trails or even learn to kayak. Picnics are always a pleasure. Pack a lunch and a blanket and head to your nearest park. Here are some other outdoor ideas: go swimming in the middle of the night; build a snowman together; take a bike ride; have a candlelight picnic in the backyard.

- Check out the museums in your area. Whatever your interests, you are sure to find a museum that matches your tastes. The next time you are out on a dinner date, stop in at a museum before going to the restaurant.

- Stay home. Build a fire, turn out the lights and talk for hours.

In a great marriage, you work together to make fun happen and do not contaminate those good times with work or family problems. I suggest you adopt a weekly *Marriage Meeting* to deal with the business side of your marital partnership. This meeting is similar to a staff meeting where you deal with such things as schedules and problem solving. There is a suggested agenda for your *Marriage Meeting* at the end of the book in the Resource Section.

DON'T GIVE UP

In 1953, a fledgling company called Rocket Chemical Company and its staff of three, set out to create a line of rust-prevention solvents and degreasers for use in the aerospace industry. It took them 40 attempts to get the water displacing formula worked out. However, they must have been really good, because the original secret formula for WD-40, which stands for *Water Displacement perfected on the 40th try*, is still in use today.[9]

Unlike these scientists and engineers, people quit too soon in many of their pursuits – jobs, school, and faith. Why? Often it's harder than they expected. It happens in marriage, too. They thought it would be easy. When it got hard, they bailed out. Any man and woman can get married. The tricky part is joyfully making it last a lifetime.

This is where it helps to have an *enduring love* in your marital tool bag. A great marriage takes time to build, as well as a tremendous effort to keep it in good shape. Working together, you can rise above the problems in your relationship and find the strength to keep trying, all because of your intense commitment to your marriage.

This sense of commitment is caught in the Biblical words of Ruth to her mother-in-law, Naomi. While they are not spoken in the context of a marriage relationship, they do express the heart of one who is committed to go the distance, no matter what.

> *Don't urge me to leave you or to turn back from you. Where you go I will go, and where you stay I will stay. Your people will be my people and your God my God. Where you die I will die, and there I will be buried. May the LORD deal with me, be it ever so severely, if anything but death separates you and me. – Ruth 1:16-17*

What's love got to do with a great marriage? A whole lot! An enduring and persevering love values the marital relationship above selfish interests. It helps you to keep working at your marriage until you get it right. Don't give up!

 TOOL TIME FOR COUPLES

1. Describe to your spouse how he or she recently practiced two of the characteristics of love listed below.

   - *Love is patient and kind.*

   - *Love is not jealous or boastful or proud or rude.*

   - *Love does not demand its own way.*

   - *Love is not irritable, and it keeps no record of when it has been wronged.*

   - *It is never glad about injustice but rejoices whenever the truth wins out.*

   - *Love never gives up, never loses faith, is always hopeful, and endures through every circumstance.*

2. Keeping love alive in marriage involves having fun together. Make a list of the things that are fun for each of you.

3. What are the obstacles to your having fun? What can you do to overcome them?

4. In the early years (or days) of your marriage, what did you do for fun? Pick one of them to repeat in the next two weeks.

CHAPTER 5

Help! We're From Different Worlds

Lisa loves her husband, Rick, but some of his personality traits make it extremely hard for her to live with him. She says, "I knew what he was like before I married him. I just thought that marriage would somehow change him. I felt he would treat me in a different way when I became his wife. After all, he said he loved me. I figured I could change him. Why can't he be like the husband he should be?" Lisa reminds me of the woman who went to her pastor to complain about her marriage. She said, "I married the ideal, but I got an ordeal. Now, I want a new deal!"

Many of us have the same frustration. You love your spouse dearly, but find it hard to live with the way he or she sometimes thinks and acts. Your spouse may be different from you, and those differences can sometimes really irk you. They can drive a wedge between the two of you and destroy the closeness you expect from your relationship. What seemed like minor quirks at first can become major points of discord in your day-to-day living.

Too many people refuse to accept their spouse as different. I learned from Dr. Gary Oliver that few people fight the law of gravity, but there are many who fight the law of differences. The alternative to accepting your spouse as *different* is to see his or her behavior as *wrong*.

> *Too many people refuse to accept their spouse as different.*

I'm not talking about ignoring or accepting bad behavior. We cannot tolerate actions that demean and harm people. I do not have the right to release rage or any other unhealthy emotion upon my spouse and tell her that she has to accept it because that's who I am. Behavior like that must be dealt with through prayer, wise counsel, repentance, and reconciliation. What I am talking about is that those unique qualities and traits of your mate, which may be driving you crazy, can be the basis for a great marriage.

THANK GOD WE'RE NOT ALIKE

We are different in the way we look, think, relate, talk, act, and approach life. That's not by accident. It's all a part of God's original design. Harold L. Myra wrote about this diversity of God's creation, including humans:

> *God's creation is remarkably diverse: from penguins to horses to Persian cats. Each feeds, mates, seeks shelter, but their sharp differences make for a fascinating world. People, too, are diverse. The principles for marriage may be the same for each couple: commitment, communication,*

shared values. But as we emphasize the commonalities,
let's equally celebrate every couple as unique.[1]

A fundamental difference is that God created us male and female – "So God created man in his own image, in the image of God he created him; male and female he created them" (Genesis 1:27). Men and women have equal value, but gender differentiates us in more than just physical ways.

Many books have been written about the way in which men and women are different. One that I especially like is *Men are Like Waffles – Women are Like Spaghetti*, written by Bill and Pam Ferrel. They are not saying that men *waffle* on decisions and are generally unstable. Instead, men approach life in what social scientists call *compartmentalizing* – putting life and responsibilities into different compartments, like the sections of a waffle. Men tend to have room for only one issue in each box. When your husband is at work, he is in the *at work box*. When he is watching TV, he is in his *watching TV box*.

Women process life more like a plate of pasta. On a plate of spaghetti, there are many individual noodles that all touch one another. The Ferrels point out that if you follow one noodle around the plate, it will intersect with other noodles, and you might even end up following another noodle. For my wife, every issue and thought is connected to every other thought and issue in some way. I sometimes get whiplash trying to keep up with her in our conversations. I respond to something she says, and find out she has already moved on to another topic. What did I miss? When did she change topics? I am a professionally trained listener. I teach other people how to listen well. This does not bode well for me. Once I asked her to give me a signal that she had moved on to another topic. She just gave me the "look." You know what I mean?

Women are usually better at multi-tasking than men. This was quite apparent at a time in our marriage when I was charged with keeping an eye on our daughters in the living room. I was reading the newspaper. Cindy was in the kitchen preparing our evening meal. You know what's coming, don't you? Sensing something was not right, Cindy walked into the living room to find our four-year-old having a great time on our beige carpet. She had taken a bowl, turned it over on the carpet, and traced several circles with crayons across the floor. Even though I was in the same room, I was totally unaware of what had occurred. I was in my *reading the newspaper box*. Cindy, on the other hand, sensed danger from another room while focused on the multiple tasks of meal preparation. How does she do that?

Our uniqueness goes beyond gender. It involves personality and preferences. We are different in how we get our energy. I am energized by being around crowds of people. Cindy is drained by crowds of people and prefers being alone. I need people; she needs privacy. Some people like to start at the beginning, taking one step at a time. When putting together a swing-set for his kids, one dad will read the instructions first. Another dad jumps in anywhere, leaps over steps, skips directions, and follows hunches. He'll look at the picture on the box and say, "I can do that!"

> *Our personality preferences color how we make decisions in our marriage.*

Our personality preferences color how we make decisions in our marriage. I tend to go by logic with a concern for truth and justice. I am good at analyzing plans, sometimes over analyzing them. Cindy tends to decide with her heart. That's not to say I am heartless or that she is not concerned for truth and justice. She is just more concerned for relationships and harmony. My preference for truth and justice did not always endear me to my children when playing board games. While they wanted to take unearned shortcuts, I insisted we play by the rules. Cindy reminded me that they were children and I should relax.

"Have a heart, Willie. They're only kids," she would say.

My response would be, "There are no shortcuts in life. They need to learn to play by the rules."

Relax, people! I am not the tin man who has no heart. It's just that I approach life with a different perspective. I have learned to balance this tendency for truth and justice with the grace that my wife brings to our marriage.

Another example of how we are different, rather than wrong, is in the way we express love to each other. Cindy and I have greatly benefited from the teachings of Dr. Gary Chapman's five love languages.[2] According to him, we all have a primary love language that fills our emotional love tanks. Here is a summary of the five love languages:

- *Physical Touch* – Some people just naturally touch the people they love. They kiss their cheek, hold their hand, or gather them up in a bear hug.

- *Words of Affirmation* – Some people find their only comfortable outlet for expressing love is in words, written or verbal.

- *Acts of Service* – Love isn't love unless it's demonstrated in practical terms (i.e. wallpapering the kitchen, washing the car, or preparing a favorite meal).

- *Gifts* – These people keep the department stores solvent. They love to buy gifts and give them to the ones they love. They also love receiving gifts, even freebies.

- *Quality Time* – They will rearrange their schedules so they can offer large blocks of time to the significant people in their lives.

What we have learned is that we tend to love each other in our own language, rather than the primary language of our spouse. I reach out and touch Cindy, when what she really wants and needs is quality time. It's not that she despises physical touch. It just doesn't mean the same to her as it does to me. Learning to understand each other's love languages has sharply improved our marriage. We celebrate these unique qualities, rather than let them divide us.

God's plan is for diversity in marriage with no division. Think of you and your spouse as two puzzle pieces fitting together, created by God to complement each other. God did not create Eve to be a female Adam, nor Adam a male Eve. They were unique, obviously different from each other. Walter Wangerin, author of *As for Me and My House*, wrote about the way some of us fight this truth:

> Some couples strain to duplicate each other, and then suffer the persistent differences or else repress them. They force unrealistic similarity upon their tastes, their opinions, their priorities, their customary habits... To make two beings carbon copies of each other is to deny...the handiwork of God. Neither person could flourish, then, and grow into the special creature God had planned him or her to be, and the marriage itself would stall.[3]

Unity, not uniformity, is God's design for dealing with differences.

Uniformity is seen at a McDonald's fast food restaurant. A hamburger in your town should taste the same as in my town. Unity, not uniformity is what God had in mind for marriage. Thank God we're not alike!

DIFFERENCES WILL NOT DESTROY YOUR MARRIAGE

Ignoring or suppressing the positive value of our differences will only heighten conflict and dissatisfaction in the marriage. People wrestle desperately to relate freely and openly. Because of the sinful nature we inherited, marriage can become a frustrated struggle – a mixture of selfishness, dissatisfaction, embarrassment, and resentment. Differences will not destroy your marriage. Instead, the *way* in which you handle these differences has a greater influence on the outcome of your marriage.

The differences that initially brought you together may be the differences that will push you away from each other.

By failing to be aware of each other's strengths and differences, we are in danger of ignoring each other's needs. Moreover, when we ignore those needs, we inflict wounds of misunderstanding, and love is not conveyed.

Misunderstandings are the result of two people seeing things differently. Your spouse may have different needs, values, life perspectives, goals, and fears. In many cases, the differences that initially brought you together may be the differences that will push you away from each other.

Gaining an understanding of how you and your spouse are different is a great tool for making a relationship work. Realizing that your spouse's actions result from his or her unique style of relating, rather than being a tactic designed to anger or offend you, changes how you view his or her behavior. It is no longer interpreted as a threat or an affront to you.

This new level of understanding leads to a relationship that is loving and kind. Paul Tournier wrote, "There is a direct link between love and understanding. It's so close that we can never be sure where one ends and the other begins, nor which of the two is the cause or the effect."[4] What is certain is that if your spouse does not feel understood, he or she will not feel accepted or loved. On the other hand, when your spouse feels loved, he or she also feels accepted and understood.

Consider what is happening in this couple's relationship. The husband enjoys long moments of quietness and time alone for thinking and meditating. His wife, however, is just the opposite. She continually has a project going and loves to cross things off her *To Do* list. When she begins to feel overwhelmed at the amount of things that she has said "yes" to, she approaches her husband for help. "Since you're not doing anything," she interrupts, "come and help me hang these pictures." Not doing anything? He is offended at that comment. How do you think he feels? He feels misunderstood and unloved.

Another couple wrestles with a different problem. He likes to do woodworking in his shop. His wife sees only the sawdust he tracks into the house that she has just spent the last three hours cleaning. He could be more careful. He doesn't understand the way in which his wife values her time, and the energy she invested in cleaning the house. The dirt doesn't bother him. It should not bother her, he reasons. How is she feeling? She feels misunderstood and unloved.

Think about your own experience. Have you ever had an intense argument with your spouse and walked away wondering what it was all about? Have you ever felt good about the way you handled a situation and then later learned that your spouse didn't like what you said or did? Do you remember the last time you were so frustrated you couldn't sleep because the person lying next to you just didn't seem to under-stand you? Taking the time to understand what you each value and need in your marriage is a tool that leads to love and acceptance.

APPRECIATE YOUR SPOUSE'S UNIQUENESS

Appreciation is another great tool for dealing with differences. It begins with an attitude that different is not bad. Rather than seeing my spouse's differences as a source of irritation and problems, I see them as opportunities for my enrichment.

I believe our differences – when understood, appreciated, and allowed to be used by God – are those things God created for the great purpose of conforming us to the image of Jesus Christ. Solomon wrote, "As iron sharpens iron, so one man sharpens another" (Proverbs 27:17). When iron pieces are rubbed in the right way, they inevitably sharpen each other, and you can expect a few sparks to fly. The process of rubbing lives together day after day becomes God's change agent, his refining tool to make us better people. This change occurs as we value each other's strengths and choose to learn from each other.

Appreciation thrives in a marital environment of unconditional love.

Appreciation thrives in a marital environ-ment of unconditional love. Often, however, we fail to love unconditionally when our spouse disappoints us by not conforming to our stan-dards. Jesus requires that we love, accept, and appreciate our spouses. He calls us to love them even when they don't measure up to either our realistic or unrealistic expectations. If we don't, they become the object of our judgment and scorn. He did not call us to change them. As much as I have tried, I have not found that command in the Bible. That's the work of the Holy Spirit in their lives.

Appreciation leads to accepting your spouse as the unique person God created, with all of his or her quirks, kinks, and idiosyncrasies. The Apostle Paul instructed the Christians in Rome to "accept one another, then, just as Christ accepted you, in order to bring praise to God" (Romans 15:7). The biblical meaning of the word "accept" is "to welcome with open arms." You are to welcome your spouse into your life and heart, without conditions. Jesus did not wait for us to become acceptable to him before he loved us. He loved us even when we were unlovable.[5]

You can accept your spouse because Christ has accepted you. You can extend to your spouse the same grace and understanding that Jesus gave you – undeserved, but freely given. This brand of acceptance is only possible when you allow God to have his way in your heart.

ADJUSTING TO YOUR SPOUSE

As you better understand your spouse and honestly appreciate his or her uniqueness, are you willing and able to adjust your relating style to meet your mate's needs? The critical issue in building a great relationship is not the compatibility of your personalities or behavioral styles. Rather, it is the commitment to understanding and adjusting to the one your heart loves.

In studying behavioral styles over the years, I've found two factors that determine how effective people are in adjusting to meet the needs of others. The first is the degree of willingness to change your behavior when appropriate, often referred to as *flexibility*. The second factor is *versatility*, which indicates a person's ability to change behavior when appropriate. Adjusting to meet your spouse's needs does not mean that you try to become a different person. You are not forsaking your true identity. You are voluntarily adjusting your behavior to meet your spouse's needs in order to build a mutually satisfying relationship. You leave the window up when you'd rather have it down. You watch someone else's favorite television show. You turn the music down when you would love to blast it. You do all of this without sighing or sulking.

Some people may be able to adjust, but are not willing to adjust, due to a lack of respect and/or trust. Still others may be willing, but don't seem to be able. Something in their background may prevent them from expressing the kind of love their spouse needs, even though they would very much like to express that kind of love. The problem may also be due to emotional immaturity and/or a lack of social skills.

You can extend to your spouse the same grace and understanding that Jesus gave you — undeserved, but freely given.

If you find it difficult to adjust your preferences to meet your spouse's needs, you may want to consider seeking help from your pastor or a competent Christian counselor. People who behave only in ways that are comfortable for them, have little potential for growth, and run the risk of creating tension and undue distress in their marriage.

A LOVING ENVIRONMENT

Creating a loving environment in your marriage requires that you shift from meeting your personal needs, to finding ways to meet your spouse's needs. You focus on the strengths of each other rather than complaining about how different you are. When you learn to appreciate the way God has wired each of you differently, love is expressed and felt.

We should ask ourselves, "What is that impulse that makes us want to redesign our spouse into our image?" It certainly isn't love. Francine Klagsbrun wrote that the strongest marriages "are those in which partners are simultaneously able to change to accommodate one another in some areas, and able to live with unchangeability in others."[6]

God wants you to honor and respect your spouse. To do less reflects a lack of God's goodness and presence in your life and marriage. If you accept your spouse only in part, you can love him or her only in part. A great marriage can happen when you see each other as different, rather than wrong.

> *Creating a loving environment in your marriage requires that you shift from meeting your personal needs to finding ways to meet your spouse's needs.*

 TOOL TIME FOR COUPLES

1. What traits of your spouse that once fascinated you now bother you? What weaknesses of your spouse that you didn't notice at first now stand out and bother you?

2. In contrast to those weaknesses, what strengths can you see in your spouse when you take the time to look for them? What are the personal contributions your spouse makes to your life for which you should regularly thank God?

3. In the course of the coming week, find ways to affirm those strengths as you relate to your spouse. For example, if one of your spouse's strengths is financial integrity, let him or her know that you really appreciate how they help you avoid overspending.

4. Discuss how accepting one another in your marriage will "bring praise to God."

CHAPTER 6

The Two-Edged Sword of Marital Communication

Cleveland Amory tells this story about Judge John Lowell of Boston. The judge was sitting at the breakfast table with his face hidden behind the morning paper. A frightened maid tiptoed into the room and whispered something into Mrs. Lowell's ear. She paled slightly, squared her shoulders resolutely, and said, "John, the cook has burned the oatmeal, and there is no more in the house. I am afraid that this morning, for the first time in seventeen years, you will have to go without your oatmeal." The judge, without putting down his paper, answered, "It's all right, my dear. Frankly, I never cared much for it anyhow."[1]

Married couples, who share the same house and bed, often discover they have grown apart, no longer sharing their intimate thoughts and feelings. They want to have great communication in their marriages, but find themselves struggling to make it happen. Communication is one of the most powerful factors influencing the quest for a great marriage. When a couple can effectively communicate with each other, they are able to solve problems, increase empathy, and develop a deeper level of friendship and intimacy.

Communication can be a two-edged sword. Through communication, either your marriage will grow, or it will be destroyed. It depends on the type of communication tools used.

WHEN LOVE TALK BECOMES BAD TALK

When couples lack the positive tools and skills for great communication, there is more *bad talk* than *love talk* in their daily lives. The use of certain negative communication tools destroys the love talk in a marriage relationship. Eliminate or keep to a minimum the bad talk in your marriage, the positive aspects of your marital love talk will blossom and grow.

> *The use of certain negative communication tools destroys the love talk in a marriage relationship.*

The importance of dealing with this bad talk is evident in this verse from the Song of Songs in the Bible, "Catch for us the foxes, the little foxes that ruin the vineyards, our vineyards that are in bloom" (Song of Songs 2:15). Foxes are sly and stealthy, often portrayed as sneaking in to steal things, such as eggs in a henhouse. In the context of a vineyard, the foxes, if given free access, will get to the ripening grapes and ruin the harvest.

In marital communication, bad talk is like the "little foxes." If you do not control the bad talk, it can erase the good effects of just about everything else you have going for you. Here is a brief listing of some of the "little foxes" that become negative communication tools:

- *Blame* – You say it's your spouse's fault and there is nothing wrong with you or with what you did.

- *Escalation* – You say or do something negative, and your spouse responds negatively. You respond to their criticism by criticizing them.

- *Painful Put-Downs* – You subtly or directly put down the thoughts, feelings, actions, or worth of your spouse.

- *Passive Aggression* – You pout, withdraw, or say nothing.

- *Hostile, Sarcastic Humor* – Your words or tone of voice communicates that you are not dealing with your conflict in an open and honest fashion.

- *Negative Interpretations* – You interpret your spouse's words or behavior more negatively than he or she intended.

- *Assumptions* – You assume you know how your spouse thinks or feels without checking it out.

- *Denial* – You insist that you don't feel angry, hurt, or sad when you really do.

- *Absolutes* – You use words like "never" and "always."

- *Fix It* – Instead of hearing the feelings of your spouse, you try to fix the problem by offering solutions. Most likely, your advice was not sought.

These negative communication tools are obvious indicators of whether you are going to have love talk or bad talk. You are doomed for failure when a conversation leads off with one of them. You might as well call a time out and start over.

POSITIVE COMMUNICATION TOOLS

Catching these little foxes before they ruin your marital vineyard increases your level of love talk. Dr. John Gottman, a marital researcher in Seattle, found that happy couples on average have five times as many positive interactions as negative interactions. This means that great marriages may not have less negativity than bad marriages, but the negativity is greatly outweighed by positive feelings and actions.[2]

A significant way of increasing those positive feelings and actions is with four communication tools found in this verse from the Song of Songs in the Bible:

> *My dove in the clefts of the rock, in the hiding places on the mountainside, show me your face, let me hear your voice; for your voice is sweet, and your face is lovely. – Song of Songs 2:14*

Tool #1: A Desire to Communicate – This attitude is lacking in many marriages. Notice what the husband says in the verse, "show me your face, let me hear your voice." He wanted her to come out from wherever she was and talk to him. He found her voice pleasing. He had a desire for communication.

A desire to communicate will result in making time to talk. One of the little foxes in so many marriages today is busyness. It is the nemesis of every marriage and it corrupts your conversations. So much of our talk takes place on the run – off to work or school or kid's games or whatever. In a national survey of married couples, researchers found that, on average, we spend less than three minutes a day in meaningful conversation.[3] Our *busy talk* tricks us into thinking that we are having meaningful conversations, when all we are trying to do is to make it to the end of the day.

Okay, you have a desire to have more than three minutes of meaningful talk during your day, but how do you do it? The obvious answer is to slow down. Benjamin Franklin said, "Lost time is never found again." Therefore, you need to focus on the present moment. It's not all about the next appointment or task. What is happening in the present moment that you don't want to miss?

The seemingly routine moments of your day can be more meaningful when you have a desire to communicate with your spouse. For instance, what's it like when you come home at the end of the day? Do you greet each other with warm words or with complaints? Did you know that the first four minutes you are together will set the tone for the rest of the evening? It's true! A loving greeting, a tender kiss, or a lingering embrace will help set the environment for love talk. One busy husband found it helpful to use his long commute home to talk to his wife on his cell phone (using the hands-free attachment, of course). They discussed the day's events and prepared to reconnect at home. It turned their previously frustrating re-entry time into a more pleasant experience.

A loving greeting, a tender kiss, or a lingering embrace will help set the environment for love talk.

Eating together is another high priority time for conversation. I'm still baffled by the numbers of couples and families that don't sit down around the table to eat. Marriage educators, Les and Leslie Parrott, note that fast food outlets have "become a mere pit stop to keep us going as we move from one activity to another."[4] *Hurry up and eat* doesn't lead to meaningful talk. A slow meal together helps you to refocus on the most important person in your life. Put off the talk about schedules, and refrain from problem solving or unpleasant topics. Talk about the personal stuff – how you are feeling, what made you happy or sad today.

Couples who find themselves with a table full of kids (or just one) might have to find an alternative to this slow type of conversation. I know about one couple who eat their meal with the whole family and then send the kids off to other parts of the house. The parents pour a cup of coffee for each other and have that slow conversation about what's happening now.

If you don't know how to start this kind of conversation, a technique we learned from Dr. Gary Chapman's marriage seminar can help. We simply ask each other this question, "What are three things that happened to you today and how did they make you feel?" Don't rush this. Having to attach a feeling to the event makes me stop and really think about it. If your spouse does not have any feelings about a certain event, don't scold him or her for it. Some of us do not attach feelings to every event in our lives. It's just something that happened, nothing more.

Do you find it hard to get excited about telling your spouse about your day? Listen to what John Maxwell did that changed his conversations with his wife at the end of the day:

> *Years ago, when something exciting happened during the day, I'd share it with colleagues and friends. By the time I got home, I had little enthusiasm for sharing it with Margaret. I purposely began keeping things to myself until*

I could share them with her first. That way she never got the leftovers.[5]

You might be eating leftovers, but you can make the conversation fresh and encouraging.

Another daily moment for meaningful conversation is before you go to sleep. Instead of dozing off with the late-night television talk shows or a book that makes you drowsy, take a few minutes to talk and pray. This does not have to be deep, deep conversation. It is definitely not a time for conflict resolution; however, it can be just a few minutes of positive affirmation, with a blessing for a peaceful night.

Speaking of grabbing moments through the day to connect, my cell phone rang as I was writing this section in my basement study. Cindy called from upstairs to tell me about two deer in our backyard. I looked out the window as she talked about how cute they were. She ended the call by saying, "I just had to share this moment with you."

Tool #2: Focused Attention – The request by the husband in Song of Songs, "Show me your face," signifies the desire for face-to-face communication. There is no hiding behind closed doors or speaking through walls. I'm not saying you can't have short bursts of conversation when in separate rooms, but you had better be sure you really heard what the other one said, or you're in big trouble.

A key to great communication is making sure you have each other's focused attention when it counts. Face-to-face conversations are better because you are able to give your attention to the verbal and non-verbal aspects of the conversation. Natural eye contact, not staring or gazing off into who-knows-where, helps you communicate that you value your spouse's words. Paying attention to your spouse's body language helps you process the words you hear, and helps your spouse make the right point. To illustrate this, look at how you can interpret the following non-verbal cues:

- Clenched Hands = anger, tension

- Crossed Arms = defensiveness, distance

- Hands on Hips = impatience

- Rubbing Neck = frustration, anger

Everything you do with your body is communicating a message whether you mean it or not. Telling your spouse, "I love you," with your hands planted on your hips sends the wrong message.

For the important talks in your marriage, find a quiet place that makes it easier to pay attention to each other, and promotes good talk rather than bad talk. If your spouse is preoccupied, don't assume that he or she is ready to listen just because you are ready to talk. Cindy and I had to work on this when I was watching mystery shows on television. Usually, the plot is resolved in the last few minutes. Sometimes there's an unexpected turn just seconds before they roll the final credits. It frustrated me – no, it made me angry – when Cindy came into the room to ask me a question during those last few scenes. It was not always a simple *yes* or *no* question, but one that required thought and an extended conversation. The result was that I missed the resolution of the mystery. As far as I was concerned, I had just wasted an hour of my life.

Everything you do with your body is communicating a message whether you mean it or not.

My wife should not have to take second place to a television show or movie, but I wanted to find out how the mystery was solved. We finally found a better way to do this. She asks if this is a good time to talk. If not, I let her know how soon I can be free, which is a win-win solution for us both. I get to see how the mystery is solved, and she knows my focused attention will soon be hers. If it's urgent, and I can usually sense that by the tone of her voice, the mystery show will have to end without my knowing the conclusion. I can catch it when they repeat it, or purchase a digital video recorder that pauses live television shows.

Tool #3: Positive Words – In the verse from Song of Songs, the husband wants to hear his wife speak. He says, "let me hear your voice; for your voice is sweet." Words are powerful when used in the context of relationships, and the Bible is clear on the effect of our words:

> *No man can tame the tongue. It is a restless evil, full of deadly poison. With the tongue we praise our Lord and Father, and with it we curse men, who have been made in God's likeness. Out of the same mouth come praise and cursing. My brothers, this should not be. – James 3:8-10*

Your words can bring blessing or cursing into your spouse's life. They can be life or death to him or her as noted in this verse, "The tongue has the power of life and death" (Proverbs 18:21). Words can help build an intimate relationship, but they can also destroy the very foundations of your marriage. Using words of blessing on a regular basis will protect your relationship from the negative emotions that sabotage a great marriage.

The sad reality is that our words are more frequently used to hurt rather than to bless. You may not feel like using positive words due to the conflict in your marriage. The last thing you want to do is *bless* your spouse; however, you have to start knocking down the walls that separate you. By using positive words, you can be the first to turn your conversations in a positive direction. Your spouse may surprise you by responding in the same way.

An example of using words to bless is seen in the words spoken by God the Father to Jesus at His baptism, "You are my Son, whom I love, with you I am well pleased" (Mark 1:11). This is a good model to follow when trying to use positive words in your marriage.

You can bless your spouse with *words of acceptance*. These words give us a sense of belonging to someone. God the Father gives Jesus the assurance, "You are my Son," claiming him as his own. This reveals that Jesus is not only the natural Son of God, but he is also the chosen Son of God.

We can communicate a lack of acceptance with careless words. I read about a husband on his honeymoon who told his new bride she had some weaknesses. Before he could list them, she responded, "Those weaknesses kept me from getting a better husband." What a way to start a marriage!

> *By using positive words, you can be the first to turn your conversations in a positive direction.*

Using *words of affection* is another way to bless your spouse. Imagine the strength of security Jesus felt as he heard the words, "You are my Son, whom I love." Tragedy stalks any relationship where belonging is without love.

I identify with the frightened little girl who was awakened in the middle of the night by thunder and lightening. As her father held her, he told her she did not need to worry because God loved her and would protect her. "I know God loves me," she said, "but right now I want someone with skin on to love me." We communicate that kind of love through our words.

The husband who stood by his wife's hospital bed after surgery is a great illustration of how to use positive words to communicate affection. Their doctor told them he had to sever a facial nerve that controlled the muscles of the wife's mouth, in order to remove a tumor. As a result, her mouth was crooked and distorted. She asked the doctor, "Will my mouth always be like this?" He said it would. The husband looked at his wife, smiled, and said that he found her mouth to be cute. Then, he bent over and kissed her, twisting his own lips to meet hers. His words matched his actions, and his wife was encouraged.[6]

A third positive way of talking is to use *words of affirmation.* Jesus heard these affirming words, "with you I am well pleased." Words of praise release a sense of confidence in our lives. The Bible reinforces the value of healthy praise. Here are two examples:

> *Do not let any unwholesome talk come out of your mouths, but only what is helpful for building others up according to their needs, that it may benefit those who listen. – Ephesians 4:29*

> *Pleasant words are a honeycomb, sweet to the soul and healing to the bones. – Proverbs 16:24*

Most of us are quick to criticize, but slow to praise. This is particularly true with those who are closest to us. When God says to his Son, "with you I am well pleased," he commends his character, honors his achievements, and encourages him for the future. Similarly, your spouse grows faster in the direction of your praise, than in the path of your criticism.

We need to be wise in how we choose and use our words. It is not necessary, nor is it wise, to say everything we are thinking. The godly wisdom of Solomon is once again helpful here, "Watch your words and hold your tongue; you'll save yourself a lot of grief" (Proverbs 21:23, MSG). A practical way of doing this is to think before you speak. I find that I can save myself a lot of grief if I think about the following questions:

- *T - Is it true?*

- *H - Is it helpful?*

- *I - Is it inspiring?*

- *N - Is it necessary?*

- *K – Can I say it in a kind way?*

To control your tongue is not easy. However, with the help of the Holy Spirit for teaching and guidance, you have a better chance at success. "It is wonderful to say the right thing at the right time!" (Proverbs 15:23, NLT).

Tool #4: Attentive Listening – People complain about their spouse's failure to express opinions and feelings, but the more frequent complaint is about a spouse who is not listening. The husband in Song of Songs invites his wife into a conversation where he wants to hear what she has to say. *Attentive listening* is probably the most important and the most difficult communication tool in our marital tool bags. Courses on the art of speaking are readily available, but the art of listening is taken for granted.

The Bible speaks about the importance of being a ready listener, giving our focused attention to the one who is speaking. "My dear brothers, take note of this: Everyone should be quick to listen, slow to speak and slow to become angry" (James 1:19).

Effective marital communication is more than just hearing the words of your spouse. Simply put, it is the process of both verbal and non-verbal sharing in such a way that your words can be accepted and understood by your spouse.

During the last 10 years of Red Auerbach's coaching career, the Boston Celtics won nine National Basketball Association championships, including a record eight straight titles from 1959 to 1966. He retired as the coach with the most wins in NBA history – 938 victories in 20 years. He also knew something about communication. He once said, "It's not what you tell your players that counts. It's what they hear."[7]

A wireless phone company has immortalized these words, "Can you hear me now?" When we say that in marriage, we mean more than, "Do you hear my words?" We want to know, "Do you understand what I mean by what I say?"

The Apostle Paul taught this communication principle when he wrote to the Corinthian church about the spiritual gifts of prophecy and speaking in tongues. "If then I do not grasp the meaning of what someone is saying, I am a foreigner to the speaker, and he is a foreigner to me" (1 Corinthians 14:11). It's not enough to just hear the words. Do I understand the meaning of the words? I may hear my wife's words, but if I fail to understand the meaning behind those words, I miss the essential transmission and reception of feelings, attitudes, facts, and beliefs that occur in great marriages.

Some of us get into trouble when we pretend to listen. This listening style fakes interest, and communicates to your spouse that what he or she has to say is not important. If what I have to say is irrelevant, then I must be unimportant. The way you listen and respond to your spouse has an effect on his or her sense of value, which can either build a fulfilling relationship or put distance between you.

Another key problem in marital communication is being misunderstood. Cindy and I were staying in a hotel many years ago when she asked, "Where did you plug in the hair dryer?" At least that's what I thought she said. You see, I was reading a magazine and heard only part of what she said. Instead of confirming what she had asked, I responded by telling her it was on the wall in front of her. She said it was not there. Now, I knew the electrical outlet had not moved since I was in there. We went back and forth with no success. Throughout this most frustrating exchange of words, I stayed on the bed trying to read my magazine. Completely irritated by my incompetence, she again asked, "Where did you put the hair dryer?" This time I actually heard her and it was not what I heard before. Having the correct information, I jumped off the bed and took it to her with numerous apologies.

Couples in great marriages learn to slow down their conversations when things start to escalate in the wrong direction.

What did I learn? First, I need to pay attention when I hear my wife's voice. Second, if we are having trouble communicating, I might have missed something.

Couples in great marriages learn to slow down their conversations when things start to escalate in the wrong direction. They paraphrase what they heard and then ask, "Have I understood your message and motive?" When you listen attentively, without interruption, and paraphrase what you heard, your spouse knows whether his or her intended message was clearly understood. It also keeps you from responding to the wrong message. Remember, be quick to listen and slow to speak.

One more thing about listening, you cannot listen well unless you close your mouth and focus on what your spouse is saying. This attentive style of listening means that when my spouse is talking, I will not be thinking about what I am going to say when she stops talking. The wisdom of the Bible emphasizes this point, "Answering before listening is both stupid and rude" (Proverbs 18:13, MSG).

COMMUNICATION IS NOT THE GOAL

There is no perfect marriage, and no amount of communication can make a marriage perfect. Dwight Small reminds us that the "glory in Christian marriage is in accepting the life-long task of making a continual adjustment within the disorder of human existence, ever working to improve communication skills necessary to this task, and seeking God's enabling power in it all."[8] You may need to exchange some of your current communication tools for ones that are more effective. It will take time to change those negative communication patterns, but with God's help, you can do it. To say that you are set in your ways, that you can't change, is to deny the power of the Holy Spirit in your life. As God's Word sinks into your heart and mind, you will be able to make the adjustments needed.

Communication is vital, but it is not the goal in a great marriage. The goal is to show your love for God and for one another. The positive tools of communication can help you achieve that goal.

 Tool Time For Couples

1. When you and your spouse have a disagreement, what usually happens? Which of the negative communication tools listed on pages 89-90 do you tend to use?

2. How could you improve the way you love your spouse with words?

3. How could you improve the way you listen to your spouse?

4. Together, decide on when you can set aside at least 10 minutes of uninterrupted time together each day to share what is going on in your lives. The focus of this time is on your feelings about each other and your life together. Discuss the following:

    ▪   What did you most enjoy about the day?

    ▪   What did you least enjoy about the day?

5. To improve your positive communication, give at least one compliment daily to your spouse that will help you focus on the strengths in your marriage. It will also highlight the positive things that attracted you to each other.

CHAPTER 7

You Spent How Much?

Ray and Donna can't remember a time when they didn't have at least one big fight every month about money. Donna had been careful about her finances all of her life. She fervently followed the rules touted by financial advisors – pay off your debt, pay yourself first, save for the future. Then, she married Ray, who thinks nothing of wasting money on his computer hobby, buying a $4 coffee, or treating friends to dinner. Their most recent clash about cash began when Donna noticed the balance on their credit card. She blamed Ray for overspending, since he made more purchases than she did.

Overspending is a common obstacle to a great marriage. Too much debt creates a strain on the family checking account. It also causes couples to spend too much time working and worrying. With the average household in America carrying a credit card debt of $9,000, both spouses are forced to work, or one spouse takes on an extra job.

The result is a lack of time and energy to build healthy relationships with each other and with their children.

Couples have trouble dealing with financial matters for a number of reasons. One spouse thinks the other one spends too much money. They disagree on how much to save and on priorities for purchases. Who controls the money is also a major battleground for a large percentage of couples.

While all couples argue about money, in some cases the arguments reveal more about the couple's ability to build a healthy relationship. Such arguments can mask larger concerns such as conflict over power and control in the marriage, differing values related to money, and a host of feelings that are associated with money for each spouse.

In the early days of our marriage, money was very tight. I was the youth pastor for a local church and Cindy was finishing her college degree. My job was our lone source of income. The only financial plan we had was to live within our means. I remember a time when I did not have any money in my wallet. That was not a good feeling. When I was invited to have lunch with a friend, I had to decline because I had no money in my wallet. When I approached Cindy to release some funds from our checking account, she saw no need for me to have this extra money. After all, she was not spending money needlessly. A full-fledged war of words followed.

If you don't learn to manage your money, it will manage you.

We did not resolve this ongoing fight until we learned that having some money in my wallet was more about independence and security than it was about buying a cup of coffee. I felt like the child having to ask the parent for money. It wasn't good for our marriage. We resolved the problem by instituting an allowance from the family account for each of us to spend or save as we pleased. It has worked for more than 30 years. Open and honest communication about these hidden issues was the first step to reducing the stress caused by money in our marriage.

Good financial management is a strategic tool for building a great marriage. If you don't learn to manage your money, it will manage you. Couples in great marriages agree on how to handle money. This chapter is not the final word on marriage and money. There are entire organizations committed to helping couples in this area.[1] I want to cover what I believe to be the foundation of financial management in a great marriage.

VALUES AFFECT MONEY DECISIONS

Money is more than paper, coins, and plastic. The way you use money reflects what is important to you, what you value. Your personal values are those qualities, situations, and material things you cherish most. Some values and attitudes toward money are traced to your childhood. What were your parents' attitudes toward money and the use of credit? Were they spenders or savers? Was money a constant point of conflict or was it a subject they never discussed openly?

We do not always adopt the same financial values as our parents. How we approach money and debt in America has changed from generation to generation. *Newsweek* magazine (August 27, 2001) told the story about three generations of one family that exposed their changing values regarding money. Frank, who was 86 years old, was committed to debt-free living. A product of the Depression, he refused to take financial risks. He paid cash for his house, and once burned a credit card mailed to him. His daughter, Linda, at age 53, had a car loan and carried a credit card balance when she had to, but paid it off quickly. For Frank's granddaughter, Jen, age 29, Grandpa's frugal financial policy was considered obsolete. She carried a credit card debt of $8,000 and a $438-a-month car loan on a $40,000 annual income. Her comment was revealing, "I don't think debt is a sin. I'm living in a style I want to become accustomed to."

In spite of what Jen believes, financial bondage does affect your relationship with God and others in a negative manner. The Apostle Paul taught this when he wrote, "For the love of money is a root of all kinds of evil. Some people, eager for money, have wandered from the faith and pierced themselves with many griefs" (1 Timothy 6:10). Billy Graham recognized this danger when he said, "There is nothing wrong with men possessing riches. The wrong comes when riches possess men."[2]

It is important for married couples to understand what money can and cannot do for them. Here is a list that I have found to be helpful:[3]

<u>What Money Can Buy</u>	<u>What Money Can't Buy</u>
A house	A home
A bed	Sleep
Books	Brains
Luxury	Culture
Medicine	Health
Flattery	Respect
Amusements	Happiness
Knowledge	Wisdom

Money can provide many things, but it cannot provide what many of us are looking for — satisfaction with one's circumstances, peace of mind, and no longer craving for things. Even people with lots of money crave more. Solomon wrote, "Those who love money will never have enough. How absurd to think that wealth brings true happiness!" (Ecclesiastes 5:10, NLT)

Once you know your core values regarding money, there are several practical principles that can help you use the financial management tool.[4]

MAINTAIN GOOD RECORDS

The number one principle of wise financial management is *to maintain good records*. You should know where your money is going. In ancient Israel, the shepherd was admonished to "know the state of your flocks" (Proverbs 27:23, NLT). He was to keep current on the condition of his livestock. I saw this principle acted out on my grandfather's farm. If one of the hogs did not show up for a feeding, he would hike into the woods to locate the missing swine. Applied to family finances, we need to be attentive to what we own, what we owe, what we earn, and where it goes. Too many couples are unaware of how much they really spend, which leads to adversity.

> *Too many couples are unaware of how much they really spend, which leads to adversity.*

As I noted in a previous chapter, we usually marry someone who has very different gifts and abilities from our own. Best-selling author and nationally syndicated radio talk show host, Dave Ramsey, notes that in marriage, "one of you is good at working numbers (the nerd) and the other one isn't good at working numbers (the free spirit). That isn't the real problem. The problem is when the nerd neglects the input of the free spirit or when the free spirit avoids participating in the financial dealings altogether."[5]

Cindy serves as the bookkeeper in our marital partnership. She loves it. I am aware of our finances, but Cindy pays the bills and maintains most of the records. With the addition of a computer to our home, I became responsible for digitizing our finances. Cindy still likes the "pencil and paper" method, but we also have the electronic backup that I create. This has helped to make us both aware of our bills.

You only need one bookkeeper in a marriage, but both of you should be well informed about your income, investments, and expenses. Research shows that couples, who feel they have equal control over money matters, are more satisfied with their marriage than couples in which one partner tends to control the finances.[6]

PLAN YOUR SPENDING

The second principle is to *plan how you spend your money*. You tell your money where you want it to go, rather than wondering where it went. It's called budgeting.

Confronted with the opportunity to purchase a truck, I sat down to see if we could afford it. I wanted it, and I wanted it badly. Cindy did not agree. Remember, she is our bookkeeper and has her finger on the pulse of our family finances. Our current vehicles were fine, but I wanted a truck. "Why do you want a truck," she asked. "So I can haul stuff," I declared.

> *You tell your money where you want it to go, rather than wondering where it went.*

After reviewing our income and current obligations numerous times, it was wretchedly apparent that I would be risking our financial strength to buy the truck. Jesus warns us, "But don't begin until you count the cost. For who would begin construction of a building without first getting estimates and then checking to see if there is enough money to pay the bills?" (Luke 14:28, NLT). Had I not taken the time to review our current situation, my wanting a truck would have brought undue stress upon our marriage.

The Bible reminds us, "Good planning and hard work lead to prosperity" (Proverbs 21:5). The opposite of good planning is impulse buying, which is when we buy too quickly. The natural-born shoppers among us should resist it. I heard of a woman who kept her credit cards in a solid block of ice in her freezer. In order to buy something for which she had no cash, she had to thaw out the cards. By the time that happened, she no longer wanted or needed what she was about to buy. It may seem like a ridiculous plan, but it's worth doing it if it will rescue your family's financial security.

Good planning also includes an agreement on the amount of money that can be spent without first checking with each other. The specific amount will depend on the budget category and your particular circumstances.

Budgeting can be difficult. It is not within the scope of this book to give details about budgeting, but I want to encourage you to devise a plan for success. It's a great feeling to know that you are in control of your money.

SAVE FOR THE FUTURE

The third financial management principle is to *save for the future*. Former television news anchor, David Brinkley, said this about the way Americans approach money, "Thrift used to be a basic American virtue. Now the American virtue is to spend money."[7] The Bible is not lacking when it comes to teaching about the value of saving money. One verse teaches, "He who gathers money little by little makes it grow" (Proverbs 13:11). Christian financial advisors recommend allocating a minimum of 10% of your income for savings and investments to help with planned and unplanned future expenses.

The envy monster is frequently the culprit that keeps us from building up our savings. We compare ourselves to others and want what they have, and we want it now! A cute phrase you may have heard sums this up, "People spend money they don't have, to buy things they don't need, to impress people they don't like."

Planning your spending helps you to save. If you live within your means, you will not be paying the exorbitant monthly credit card interest rates that result from paying only the minimum monthly amount. That means you will have money to put into savings, even if it is a small amount. It is never too late, or too early, to start saving and investing for the future.

Another enemy of saving for the future is instant gratification. We do not want to wait for that which we cannot afford now. Easy credit has made instant gratification a national pastime. Before buying something you can't afford, try asking yourself the following questions:[8]

- *Is this a need? Want? Or desire?*

- *Am I getting the best deal I can for the money?*

- *Does it reflect the Lord in me?*

- *Will it accomplish God's purpose?*

- *What is my goal?*

- *Will this purchase require extra time for upkeep?*

- *Will it hold its value?*

- *Is this an instant decision? An unplanned item?*

- *Is this a get-rich-quick thing?*

- *Have I prayed about this?*

- *Did my spouse ask for this?*

Planning for the future involves discussing long-range plans with your spouse. This would include the children's college educations and marriages, your retirement, and what to do in the event that one of you dies before the other.

ENJOY WHAT YOU HAVE

The fourth principle of good financial management is to *enjoy what you have.* This is the principle of contentment as taught in this Bible verse, "Keep your lives free from the love of money and be content with what you have, because God has said, 'Never will I leave you; never will I forsake you'" (Hebrews 13:5). A cartoon pictured a married couple standing next to a glistening new car in an auto dealer's showroom. The wife is busily punching the keypad of her handheld calculator. The irritated husband says, "Now, dear, you know we need a new car. Stop trying to figure out how many starving children we could feed if we drive the old clunker another year." This illustrates the dilemma in which we sometimes find ourselves – a struggle between what we want and what we should do.

> *Contentment rather than out of control consumption is a better testimony of God's presence in our homes.*

Contentment and satisfaction in life have nothing to do with money and everything to do with your relationship with God. I like the wisdom of this particular proverb, "Don't weary yourself trying to get rich. Why waste your time? For riches can disappear as though they had the wings of a bird!" (Proverbs 23:4-5, NLT). Why chase after something that can just fly away? True, lasting contentment is learned through trusting God for our daily needs and living within our means.

Financial contentment comes when we see money as God sees it. Ron Blue has a great way of summarizing the way money is viewed by God, "Money is a tool God uses to mold us to His image. It is a test of our faithfulness (Luke 16:11-13). And it is a vehicle that can enhance our individual testimonies; it provides opportunities for us to be salt and light to this world (Matthew 5:13-16)."[9]

A lack of contentment among Christian families does restrict resources that can be used by local churches and ministries in advancing the Kingdom of God. Jesus taught, "Where your treasure is, there your heart will be also" (Matthew 6:21). Contentment, rather than out of control consumption, is a better testimony of God's presence in our homes.

GIVE BACK TO GOD

The final principle is to *give back to God,* the standard of tithing a portion of your income to your church and Christian ministries. The Bible abounds with examples and commands regarding how we are to honor the Lord with our finances. Among them is this one, "Honor the LORD with your wealth, with the firstfruits of all your crops" (Proverbs 3:9). It is clear that God does not want the leftovers.

Christians unable to give freely to God's work, regardless of the amount, are often in financial bondage. In the first year of our marriage, Cindy and I did not always give back to God before we gave to anyone else. I remember times when we held back our church giving in order to pay the electric bill, or the gas bill, or some other earthly encumbrance. We never seemed to get caught up on our giving to God. Then we decided to give 10% of our income, a tithe, to God right off the top of each paycheck, our "firstfruits." We would trust him to provide enough for us to live on. We have never regretted that decision.

By first giving to God, Cindy and I know that all we have is by his grace, and that we are to be good stewards of what he entrusts to us. The real question is not, "How much are we going to give to God?" Rather, it is, "How much of God's money are we going to spend on ourselves?"

MONEY IS DANGEROUS

There is nothing immoral about possessing money or material goods. However, pursuing wealth for the sake of pleasure, or for meeting emotional needs, or to keep up with friends, leads to family friction, personal discontent, and spiritual compromises. When money becomes the focus of your marriage, you are in trouble. Marital conversations become more about how to pay the next bill than about how much you love each other. Resentments can simmer and fester until they explode in a furious rampage.

You can avoid these dangerous situations by using the financial principles in this chapter. The results will be financial freedom and a more rewarding family life. They will help you avoid the pain so many couples are experiencing in their marriages. Use your money wisely to build a great marriage.

 TOOL TIME FOR COUPLES

1. What are your core values about money? In other words, what do you believe about the role of money in your marriage – how it is earned, saved, and spent? For example, a core value might be, "I believe that the money we each earn should be combined into one account." On separate sheets of paper, list what you each believe about the use of money in marriage.

2. Take some time to decide on your core money values as a couple. Compare your individual values from the exercise above. Where do you agree? How can you negotiate your differences? On a separate sheet of paper, list the core values that will guide your use of money as a couple. Place the list in a place that will be visible and remind you of what you have decided.

3. Do you agree (A) or disagree (D) with the following statements? Circle the appropriate letter.

<u>Husband</u>   <u>Wife</u>

A D	1.	We have a specific plan for how much money we can spend each month.	A D
A D	2.	I am satisfied with our decisions about how much money we should save.	A D
A D	3.	We handle credit wisely.	A D

114

A   D   4. We do not have problems deciding what   A   D
               is most important to spend money on.

A   D   5. We keep good records regarding our fin-   A   D
               ances.

A   D   6. We give generously to our church and   A   D
               other ministries.

4. Compare and discuss your answers with your spouse.

5. What steps can you take that would enable you to change a "D" answer to an "A" answer? Discuss with your spouse how to implement this plan.

CHAPTER 8

Ground Rules for a Fair Fight

I will forever remember the elderly couple sitting in the car in front of us at the traffic light. They were having a lively conversation, and I imagined what must have been going on between them. Perhaps she was reminiscing about the success of their long years together. Maybe he was delighting in the exploits of their grandchildren. Without warning, she attacked the man behind the wheel with her purse. A few unheard words from him, and the purse furiously came at him again. The only thing that saved that poor man was when the traffic light turned green. They drove off, never to be seen by me again.

CONFLICT IS INEVITABLE

You don't have to be married very long before you start tripping over a few relational snags. There is conflict in the best of marriages.

We've all experienced the pain of hurt and disappointment due to marital conflict. When I hear married couples say that they never have any conflicts, I assume one of several possibilities:

- *They have not been married very long.*

- *They don't know each other very well.*

- *They don't talk to each other very much.*

- *They are lying!*

Gary Thomas suggests a couple of other reasons in his book, *Sacred Marriage*, "The absence of conflict demonstrates that either the relationship isn't important enough to fight over or that both individuals are too insecure to risk disagreement."[1] Conflict is painful. It brings out anger, fear, and anxiety, all of the emotional experiences we try to avoid.

Not all conflict is bad. It can provide an opportunity for growth in a relationship. Like dynamite, it is helpful if used right, but destructive if used at the wrong time, or in the wrong manner. Through healthy conflict, couples learn to appreciate, understand, and accept other points of view. They focus on how to manage conflict successfully when it does arise.

COMBAT IS OPTIONAL

As noted above, conflict in marriage is unavoidable, but combat is optional. When hurt or offended by your spouse, you have at least three response options: revenge, ignore the offense, or face the anger and hurt so you can resolve the conflict.

Revenge has never been a good option. It may be sweet for the moment, but the long-term result is not so pleasurable. Be careful about revenge. Strange things can happen. Tommy Nelson, pastor of the Denton Bible Church (Denton, TX), tells this priceless story about revenge in marriage:

A woman asked her husband one morning to zip up the back of her dress. He began to play around with the zipper in a flirtatious way, zipping it up and down, up and down. In the process, the zipper broke. She had just had the dress dry-cleaned and was late for a meeting, and there she stood with a "broken" dress. She was furious.

About 5:30 that evening, she returned home, still angry over her husband's behavior that morning. She found her husband working on his car, lying underneath the car from his waist up, the lower part of his body sticking out and temptingly accessible. He didn't seem to hear her as she approached, so she reached down, grabbed the zipper on the front of his jeans, and began to zip it up and down, just as he had done with her dress that morning. Then she walked into the house.

To her astonishment, her husband was standing in the kitchen. She said, "What are you doing in here?" He said, "What do you mean? It's our kitchen."

She said, "You were under the car just two seconds ago."

"No," he said, "I haven't been under the car at all."

"Well, who is out there in our garage working under your car?"

"It's the next-door neighbor," he said. "The muffler was coming off and he volunteered to fix it, so I told him I'd really appreciate his help and I came in here to fix a glass of tea for him when he's finished."

His wife went pale as a white sheet. She admitted to her husband what she had done, and they both hurried out to apologize to the man. They found the guy lying totally still. He didn't respond to their calls, so they pulled him out from under the car by his legs. When he came to, they discovered that he had done what any man would have done if someone suddenly grabbed the zipper to his pants. He sat straight up, and bam, he hit his head on the underside of the car with such force that he knocked himself out!

This story is humorous, but revenge is not usually a laughing matter. An angry spouse may withhold intimacy, affection, or kindness as a means of revenge. The desire to get even has led to bankruptcy, adultery, and abuse.

A second option in conflict is to ignore the offense or hurt. There may be times when this is appropriate. Your spouse is having a bad day and you know that he or she is not intentionally trying to hurt you. My good friends, John and Brenda Buck, gave me this advice, "You don't have to go to every fight you're invited to." There are times when it may be wise to ignore a conflict because you don't know how to resolve it without creating an even bigger conflict. However, denying your anger, holding it in, or never expressing it to your spouse, leads to resentment, hate, and revenge. The inevitable result is a violent explosion of words, and sometimes, physical abuse. All of your unresolved anger spews out without regard for how it wounds and pushes your spouse even farther from you. One of the most destructive things that can happen to a marriage is to have the growing sense that you are living in a minefield.

It doesn't have to be this way, or ever get to be this way in the first place. There is a third option for dealing with marital conflict. You can face the anger and hurt so that you can resolve the conflict in a healthy manner. How can you do that? Based upon more than 35 years of marriage and working with married couples, I have found some ground rules that can keep your conflicts from turning into nasty, knockdown, drag-out fights.

RULE #1: ADOPT A NO-LOSERS POLICY

The first thing you do is *adopt a no-losers policy.*[3] The eighteenth-century French philosopher, Joseph Joubert, said, "The aim of an argument or discussion should not be victory, but progress." When one spouse in a marriage loses, both spouses lose. A no-losers policy helps you work toward mutual understanding, and a win-win solution about which both you and your spouse feel good.

In great marriages, couples recognize the enormous value of teamwork and each spouse is committed to working on cooperative strategies. A marriage begins to die when selfishness replaces teamwork as the motivation for resolving disagreements. The setting aside of our own agenda, for the benefit of our spouse, is required at significant moments in marriage. The Apostle Paul said, "Don't push your way to the front; don't sweet-talk your way to the top. Put yourself aside, and help others get ahead. Don't be obsessed with getting your own advantage. Forget yourselves long enough to lend a helping hand" (Philippians 2:3-4, MSG).

A marriage begins to die when selfishness replaces teamwork as the motivation for resolving disagreements.

Hard pushing competiveness may help you become the sales person of the month, land that new job, or win a sports contest; however, it will not help you build a great marriage. Power struggles in marriage are destructive. Why? In every power struggle, people become adversaries, trying to crush their opponent. You view your spouse as the enemy who must be defeated at all costs.

Your spouse is not your enemy! Zig Ziglar, a popular motivational speaker, once quipped, "Many marriages would be better if the husband and wife clearly understood that they are on the same side."[4] God's plan for a great marriage is for husbands and wives to be a team, united in accomplishing his purposes in marriage. Jesus emphasized this marital unity in one of his conversations with the Pharisees:

> *Haven't you read...that at the beginning the Creator "made them male and female," and said, "For this reason a man will leave his father and mother and be united to his wife, and the two will become one flesh"? So they are no longer two, but one. Therefore what God has joined together, let man not separate. – Matthew 19:4-6*

Dr. Howard Hendricks, a noted author and speaker, said that one of the things he learned from working with the Dallas Cowboys was the importance of the team. "When you are on a team," he said, "you play off the strengths of your teammates. You don't tackle the guys who wear the same color uniforms."

Having to win every argument will wear you down physically, emotionally, and spiritually. It will also destroy your marriage. A better way is to approach your disagreements with a desire to protect what's great about your marriage from whatever problem you are facing at the time.

RULE #2: KEEP IT HONEST, TEMPERED WITH LOVE

The second ground rule is to *speak honestly, but temper it with love.*

In times of conflict, we can retreat into philosophical exchanges of ideas, instead of expressing our real feelings. We mask our feelings with cerebral-sounding theories like, "I think you are just projecting your latent hostilities onto my behavior." Alternatively, we deny the truth by saying, "I'm not angry. I'm actually quite calm and rational about this matter." We learn from God's Word that it is important to express our feelings and thoughts honestly and appropriately:

> *The Lord detests lying lips, but he delights in men who are truthful.* – Proverbs 12:22

> *Therefore each of you must put off falsehood and speak truthfully to his neighbor, for we are all members of one body. "In your anger do not sin": Do not let the sun go down while you are still angry, and do not give the devil a foothold.* – Ephesians 4:25-27

This kind of conversation begins by stating your perception of the problem in a non-accusatory manner. If you are upset that your spouse fails to let you know that he or she will be late, you could say, "When you don't call, I feel worried and upset because I imagine how terrible it would be if something happened to you." The value of this approach is that you quickly get to what really bothers you, and your spouse is less likely to be defensive.

Keeping it honest, tempered with love, involves expressing your anger in healthy ways. Anger is not always wrong; however, the Bible warns us to avoid the sinful temper explosions, the anger that plans to hurt your spouse, and the putrid words that injure the spirit. The influence of your speech is noted in this verse, "The tongue has the power of life and death" (Proverbs 18:21a). When we attack the person rather than the problem, we move into deadly areas. Calling each other derogatory names, no matter how creative, is not going to help you overcome the problem facing you.

Anger is a secondary emotion, resulting from disappointment about the past, or frustration about something in the present, or fear of the future.

A better method is to locate the source of your angry feelings and express them in a healthy way. Anger is a secondary emotion, which results from disappointment about something in the past, or frustration about something in the present, or fear of something in the future. A healthy expression of anger includes a clear statement of how you are feeling now. You can say, "I'm frustrated because you don't do what I ask you to do. It makes me feel like you don't respect me." That is much better than, "You make me so angry!" Blaming your spouse is one of the largest factors in causing imbalance in marriages, and it keeps the anger going. Locating the true source of your anger, and taking personal responsibility for your feelings is a major step towards resolving your marital conflicts.

RULE #3: KEEP SHORT ACCOUNTS

The third ground rule is to *keep short accounts with each other*. Based on this admonition in the Bible, "Do not let the sun go down while you are still angry" (Ephesians 4:26), you deal with the issue quickly, openly, forthrightly, and head-on. Some couples mistakenly think this verse means that they have to stay up all night until the matter is settled. That only makes the conflict worse in some cases. It is better to deal with your conflicts on a daily basis, if possible. The longer you wait to get a matter off your chest, the bigger the problem becomes. There is nothing good about a prolonged conflict.

Timing is critical. Choosing a time that will allow for the greatest understanding and team effort is very important. If you are hungry, tired, emotionally upset, or have limited time before an ap-
pointment, choose another time to deal with the conflict. The word "later" is not adequate because you each may have a different idea of when you will get together. Agree to a specific time. This demonstrates your willingness to work on the problem. You also allow your-

> *The longer you wait to get a matter off your chest, the bigger the problem becomes.*

selves time to think through what the real issue is and how you each feel about it.

In order to keep short accounts, you and your spouse must agree on how to solve your relational problems effectively. Here are some key suggestions:

Identify the real problem. – Dr. Gary Smalley says, "The external prob-
lem is rarely the problem."[5] The surface issues of many marital arguments are fueled by fears and needs that are not readily seen. Cindy and I once had an intense argument before leaving home on one of our wedding anniversaries. We would be gone overnight, and she wanted to know how much food I had left for our cats to eat. My answer was, "Enough." She repeated her question and I repeated my answer, adding a little more volume. We continued this for a few rounds until I walked away.

What was the problem? Why couldn't I just tell her how much cat food was in the dish? Eventually, we figured out that the real problem was my fear of being controlled and my fear of inadequacy. Once I realized she was not trying to control me, nor was she viewing me as an inadequate husband, we have not argued about how much food is in

the cat's dish. You will be more effective in problem solving as you take the time to define the real problem or conflict issue.

Listen to how each of you feels about the problem. – This may be the last thing you want to do when you are fuming about what has happened. However, nothing is more powerful in producing a positive resolution to the conflict.

Roger and Joyce were at odds over how to handle their five-year-old son's unwillingness to put away his toys and pick up his room. Joyce thought that if he did not change, he would pick up some bad habits. On the other hand, Roger's opinion was that their son was simply going through a phase that would disappear, if they didn't make a big deal of it. Here is what they said to each other during this stage of trying to resolve their differences:

> Joyce: *"I can't stand his messes anymore. I feel as if my full-time job is picking up after him."*
>
> Roger: *"It sounds like you are angry because you have to pick up after him."*
>
> Joyce: *"Yes, and I'm also angry at you for not making him do it. It seems to me that you just don't care."*

In this conversation, Roger used his positive communication tools to listen to how Joyce felt about the issue. He focused on trying to understand her rather than presenting his side. He got his turn after she was sure that he understood her view.

Be clear about your concern, but avoid being critical. – You cross the line when you add on negative words about your spouse's character or personality. It is better to share your concern without throwing in blame and character assassination. Marital researcher, John Gottman, gives this example of the way a legitimate complaint or concern can be turned into a criticism:

- Concern: "*You were supposed to check with me before inviting anyone over for dinner. I wanted to spend time alone with you tonight.*"

- Criticism: "*Why do you keep putting your friends ahead of me? I always come last on your list. We were supposed to have dinner alone tonight.*"⁸

Take responsibility for your own contribution to the conflict. – Maybe you have ignored your spouse's previous attempts to resolve this issue, or you have made unreasonable demands on your spouse. For you to have a great marriage, it is essential that both of you take responsibility for your own actions that have not led to positive changes.

Ask God for His opinion. – Taking time to pray for wisdom from God is a great way to get your heart in the right attitude. The Bible says, "So let us come boldly to the throne of our gracious God. There we will receive his mercy, and we will find grace to help us when we need it" (Hebrews 4:16, NLT). Bringing God into this process is a significant way to distinguish you from non-Christian couples. Here is how one couple does this:

First, we always pray and tell God that we want to follow his will for our lives. Then we look hard at the Bible to see what it says about our situation. We don't argue about what I want or what he wants. Sometimes we can't agree on what God wants, but we leave it up to God to show us through the Bible or through the other ways he can guide us, like prayer and wise Christian counsel.

Brainstorm about a win-win solution. – Work as a team to come up with as many possible specific and positive solutions as you can. Most relational problems have more than one solution. The more possible solutions you have, the more likely you will find one that both of you will accept. It is crucial that you do not criticize any ideas in the brainstorming stage. Try to be creative and keep track of the suggestions.

Select a win-win solution. – You can now discuss the pros and cons of the different potential solutions. If one spouse likes an idea, but the other spouse finds it unacceptable, take time to discuss the reasons. The communication tools covered in Chapter 6 will be helpful here. The goal is to work toward what you both agree you will try to do.

Implement your solution. – Focus on your own behavior and let your spouse work on his or her changes.

Evaluate and rework your solution if necessary. – Agree on an adequate amount of time to try your solution. At the end of that period, meet together to discuss how your plan is working or not working. If it's not working, go back to the discussion phase at the beginning.

What happens if you fail to work as a team during this process? You will get stuck and start spinning your wheels. This is often a sign that you, or your spouse, were not completely honest with each other during the discussion phase at the beginning. When this happens, go back to the beginning. Don't give up. If you are unable to find a workable solution together, it may be time to talk with your pastor, a trained marriage mentor couple, or a professional counselor.

RULE #4: FOCUS ON GRACE RATHER THAN REVENGE

The last ground rule for a fair fight is to *focus on grace rather than revenge*. Even in the moments of anger, betrayal, exasperation, and hurt, God wants you to pursue your spouse with the goal of reconciling and embracing him or her with his love that is in you.

The Bible commands us, "Get rid of all bitterness, rage and anger, brawling and slander, along with every form of malice. Be kind and compassionate to one another, forgiving each other, just as in Christ God forgave you" (Ephesians 4:31-32). This is what Gary and Barbara Rosberg call, "forgiving love." The Rosbergs believe that "forgiving love heals hurts and helps spouses feel accepted and connected."[7] It offers a fresh start after you have offended and hurt each other. The absence of forgiving love pushes you apart. You may even use your spouse's sins to justify pulling away from him or her.

Evelyn and James Whitehead wrote, "The challenge is not to keep on loving the person we thought we were marrying, but to love the person we did marry!"[8] *Forgiving love* may be the most difficult marital tool to use, but the benefits far outweigh the effort.

I met Barbara and Ben a few years ago at a challenging time in their marriage. Barbara had become involved in an emotional affair with a work associate and wondered if Ben would ever get over her misdeed. Just when she thought it was safe and things were getting better, something would trigger his verbal assaults, leaving her emotionally hemorrhaging. "Why can't he forgive me and move on?" she asked. The answer to her question is that

> *Forgiveness is often a process rather than a one-time event.*

forgiveness is often a process rather than a one-time event. More often than not, we must relinquish our bitterness a dozen times or more, continually choosing to release the offender from our judgment.[9]

Married couples often misunderstand biblical forgiveness. It is not simply saying, "I forgive you", and moving on. Dr. Lewis Smedes, an author and seminary professor, helps explain what forgiveness is and is not:

- *When we forgive a person, this does not mean we are immediately healed.*

- *When we forgive a person, this does not mean we are going to be buddy/buddy.*

- *When we forgive a person, this does not mean that we trust them, yet.*

- *When we forgive a person, we are not avoiding pain; we are opening the door to healing.*

- *When we forgive a person, this does not mean we surrender the right to restitution or justice when appropriate.*

- *When we forgive, we take the journey at the pace we are able to handle...the deeper the hurt, the longer the journey.[10]*

Let's get back to Ben and Barbara. He was hurt deeply by his wife's actions. He wondered if he could ever trust her again. Barbara just wanted to get on with the marriage. She apologized more than once for her actions, but Ben needed to work through his hurt. He was not convinced that she fully understood how deeply she had hurt him and that he needed time to process it. Dr. David Stoop, a clinical psychologist, warns against instant forgiveness in certain situations. He counsels, "Quick forgiveness can be interpreted by the other person as meaning *no big deal*, which for some can be an invitation to continue the hurtful behavior."[11]

Ben struggled to forgive his wife. "I know I'm a Christian," he said, "but she did an awful thing to me and our marriage. I just can't forgive and forget."

"Are you sure you can't forgive her, or do you mean you will not forgive her?" I asked. "Often when we say, *I can't*, we really mean, *I won't*."

He thought about it for a few moments. "You're right," he confessed. "I don't want to forgive her."

I told Ben that there are many good reasons to practice forgiving love in marriage. Here they are:

- Jesus commanded us to do so. "If you hold anything against anyone, forgive him" (Mark 11:25).

- Not doing so hinders your relationship with God; it puts you out of fellowship with Him. "Forgive him, so that your Father in heaven may forgive you your sins" (Mark 11:25).

- You forgive because you have personally experienced God's grace and forgiveness. "Shouldn't you have had mercy on your fellow servant just as I had on you?" (Matthew 18:33)

- To forgive is a powerful way to be like Jesus. "Bear

with each other and forgive whatever grievances you may have against one another. Forgive as the Lord forgave you" (Colossians 3:13).

Forgiveness is not just good for our souls. It is also good for our bodies. People who forgive benefit from better immune functioning and lower blood pressure. They have better mental health than people who do not forgive, and feel better physically. They also experience lower amounts of anger and fewer symptoms of anxiety and depression. All of this results in more satisfying, longer-lasting relationships.

Resolving marital feuds is neither simple, nor easy; however, one of the quickest ways to end a fight is to admit when you are wrong, and seek forgiveness.

Barbara and Ben did reconcile their marriage. He forgave her, and started working on building a restored relationship with her. She recognized her own contributions to the trouble in their marriage and apologized. By focusing on grace rather than revenge, and finding the courage to forgive and reconcile their differences, Barbara and Ben are well on their way to building a great marriage.

IT'S NOT THAT SIMPLE

In the hit movie, *Home Alone*, eight-year-old Kevin found himself sitting in church beside his elderly neighbor, a bedraggled old man who was the subject of frightening rumors among the neighborhood children. The man was there during his granddaughter's Christmas choir rehearsal because he knew he would not be welcomed during the performance. Years before, he and his son had a grievance that erupted into harsh words and flailing fists. The old man was not allowed to see his beautiful granddaughter, so he sneaked in when he would not be noticed. Sensing his anguish and pain, Kevin asked him this simple question: "Why don't you just go to your son and tell him you're sorry?" The old man mumbled that it was not that simple, and left.

Resolving marital feuds is neither simple, nor easy; however, one of the quickest ways to end a fight is to admit when you are wrong, and seek forgiveness. The goal is not to win an argument. The goal should always be to heal the relationship. To seek a solution that will result in a stronger marriage, greater understanding, and a deeper love often involves the giving and receiving of forgiveness.[12]

Focusing on grace and forgiveness keeps bitterness, revenge, and anger from destroying your marriage.

Forgiving love is a power tool in marriage. It frees you for a restored relationship with your spouse, because you choose not to hold it against her or to get even with him. Depending on the magnitude of the offense, you may not be able to eradicate it from your memory, but you can choose not to dwell on it. Focusing on grace and forgiveness keeps bitterness, revenge, and anger from destroying your marriage. It is not easy by any stretch of the imagination. As we give to one another the acceptance and forgiveness that God has given to us, he brings that same redemption into our marriages. In bearing with one another and covering each other's sin with grace, God touches our lives together with healing.

THE FORGIVENESS DATE

Several years ago, I developed what I called, "The Forgiveness Date." It is a tool that can help couples reconcile their relationships. It is not necessary to use it for the offenses that can be handled with a quick apology. It is a more structured strategy that is needed for those transgressions that create deep emotional and relational rifts in your marriage. For those times, the following steps can be beneficial:

STEP ONE – Decide to work on the issue in question. This is an act of your mind and heart to move towards reconciliation.

STEP TWO – Pray together for the Lord to bless your time discussing this issue. In this step, you are preparing your heart for reconciliation.

STEP THREE – Explore the pain and concerns of the offended person. Let the offended spouse share how he or she has been hurt. The offending spouse paraphrases what he or she understands their spouse to be saying. Do not rebut. The goal is to validate the offended spouse's feelings.

STEP FOUR – The offender apologizes and asks for forgiveness. Authentic reconciliation is a two-person transaction that is made possible by apologies. How you apologize and what you say in the apology is important. In their research and interaction with hundreds of individuals, Dr. Jennifer Thomas and Dr. Gary Chapman, authors of *The Five Languages of Apology*, have discovered five fundamental aspects of an apology:[13]

- *Expressing Regret – "I am sorry."*

- *Accepting Responsibility – "I was wrong."*

- *Making Restitution – "What can I do to make it right?"*

- *Genuinely Repenting – "I'll try not to do that again."*

- *Requesting Forgiveness – "Will you please forgive me?"*

As you consider what your spouse has said, it may be necessary to use more than one of these languages of apology. Find the one that best communicates your apology to your spouse.

STEP FIVE – The offended spouse agrees to forgive, "just as in Christ God forgave you" (Ephesians 4:32). This kind of forgiveness means you give up your perceived right to get even. The Bible admonishes us, "Do not repay anyone evil for evil" (Romans 12:17). After forgiving your spouse, try to move ahead constructively with the relationship, recognizing that real love "always hopes, always perseveres" (1 Corinthians 13:7).

STEP SIX – You both commit the issue to the past. You don't hold it over your partner's head. Remember that biblical love "keeps no record of wrongs" (1 Corinthians 13:5). It's not fair to throw the issue at your spouse in a future conflict.

STEP SEVEN – Pray together for grace to release the issue as a barrier between you. The following Bible verse explains the value of this action:

> *Make this your common practice: Confess your sins to each other and pray for each other so that you can live together whole and healed. The prayer of a person living right with God is something powerful to be reckoned with. – James 5:16, MSG*

You Always Have a Choice

Conflict is inevitable in a great marriage, but combat is optional. You always have a choice in how you deal with your anger, fear, and anxiety. Choosing to implement these ground rules allows you to control the conflicts and disagreements in your marriage, rather than having them control you.

 TOOL TIME FOR COUPLES

1. Reflect on a recent disagreement you had as a couple. Did you resolve it adequately? If not, discuss how the ground rules in this chapter would have helped you.

2. Go over the *Ground Rules for a Fair Fight* together, one at a time. Discuss the following questions to see how each rule will benefit you. Modify any rules you need to, so that they will help you the most.

   - What are the positive things about this ground rule? Are there any negatives?

   - What do we like about this ground rule? What don't we like?

3. Do you need to plan a "Forgiveness Date?" When will you do it?

CHAPTER 9

Great Sex in a
Great Marriage

I heard the popular humorist, Garrison Keillor, tell the story about what happened between Ole and Lena on the night of their 25th wedding anniversary. They had returned home from a nice dinner and were sitting on the couch. Without warning, Lena punched Ole in his shoulder. "What's that for?" he asked. "That's for 25 years of bad sex," she said.

Ole sat there for a while trying to figure out his response. He then punched Lena in her shoulder. Completely caught off guard, she asked, "What's that for?" To which Ole responded, "That's for knowing the difference!"

Many couples have let the passion of sexual intimacy diminish in their marriage. They have settled for less delight in their marriage beds. According to a national survey conducted by Life Innovations, the most problematic sexual issue for couples is dissatisfaction with the amount of affection received.[1]

The *urge to merge* is from God, who intends it to be a fulfilling experience in marriage. Great sex does not begin with soft lights, mood music, perfect bodies, and all the right moves. In a great marriage, sex begins with right thinking in your mind about marital intimacy.

HOW DO YOU SPELL INTIMACY?

Men tend to define intimacy as some form of action, such as sexual intercourse, participating together in a recreational activity, and physically doing something for his wife. As one husband said to his wife, "What do you mean we need more intimacy? I just built you a gazebo!"

When you can relax and feel safe with each other, the stage is set for a more meaningful love life.

That action increased the emotional bond he felt with his wife. He would not have done that for just any woman.

Women tend to view intimacy as the sharing of an emotional bond, warmth, closeness, and vulnerability. This is accomplished most often through meaningful heart-to-heart conversations. One wife complained about her husband when she said, "He tells me things that sound like a news report rather than loving thoughts." A man who is open about his own thoughts and feelings creates an emotional bond with his wife.

This difference between the sexes undeniably influences the physical expression of intimacy in marriage. David Olson, one of the authors of *Empowering Couples*, summarizes it this way, "Feelings of emotional intimacy in the relationship usually precede sexual expression for women, whereas males often view sex as a way to increase intimacy."[2] This dissimilarity is responsible for more than a few marital skirmishes.

Rather than ignoring or fighting these differences, couples in great marriages are proactive in building the emotional bond in their marriage. When you can relax and feel safe with each other, the stage is set for a more meaningful love life.

SEXUAL PLEASURE

Let's get more specific about what God has to say on the subject of sex in marriage. In his infinite wisdom, God personally and lovingly created us male and female. He designed us so that we could enjoy within marriage the complete expression of the sexual dimension. The marriage bed is to be honored and enjoyed by both husband and wife without guilt or restraint.

God designed the expression of marital intimacy for more than the enlargement of the family. As a part of his good creation, God designed sexual pleasure for marriage. Proverbs instructs husbands to "rejoice in the wife of your youth…may her breasts satisfy you always, may you ever be captivated by her love" (Proverbs 5:18-19). Gary Thomas, writing in *Sacred Marriage*, made one of the clearest comments I have found about how God created our bodies for physical pleasure:

> *God made flesh, and when God made flesh, he created some amazing sensations. While the male sexual organ has multiple functions, the female clitoris has just one – sexual pleasure. By design, God created a bodily organ that has no other purpose than to provide women with sexual ecstasy. This wasn't Satan's idea – it was God's. And God called every bit of his creation "very good" (Genesis 1:31)…The reason it feels good is because God designed it so.[3]*

The marriage bed should be fun! Some people are so serious about *the objective*; they have lost the fun of the relationship. Grins, giggles, and laughter ought to be a part of your sexual intimacy.

THE PRINCIPLE OF SATISFACTION

Have you approached sex in marriage as something you deserve and want, or have you approached sex as a very wonderful way to please your spouse like no other person can? The marriage bed is for the expression of unselfish affection. It's not all about you and your orgasm. Great sex in marriage happens when you focus on how to satisfy your spouse. This is the essence of what I call, *The Principle of Satisfaction*, which is found in this passage from Paul's first letter to the Corinthians:

> *The marriage bed must be a place of mutuality - the husband seeking to satisfy his wife, the wife seeking to satisfy her husband. Marriage is not a place to "stand up for your rights." Marriage is a decision to serve the other, whether in bed or out. – 1 Corinthians 7:3-4, MSG*

As you can see, the Bible teaches that marital intimacy is not just for your satisfaction. You are to discover what pleases your spouse and delight in fulfilling those desires. This means the marriage bed can still be exciting after many years of marriage because the husband and wife are still learning how to please one another.

The Principle of Satisfaction is also highlighted in the Old Testament book, Song of Songs, as seen in these verses:

> *Let him kiss me with the kisses of his mouth – for your love is more delightful than wine. – Song of Songs 1:2*

> *How delightful is your love, my sister, my bride! How much more pleasing is your love than wine. – Song of Songs 4:10*

The love in these verses refers to a married couple's physical intimacy – their caresses, embraces and consummation. These expressions of love were more delightful and more pleasing to them than any other experience in their lives. I was teaching on this topic in a marriage seminar and asked the couples to tell their spouses what they would substitute for wine in those passages. A husband later told me that his wife looked alluringly at him and whispered the word, "chocolate." He was already thinking of some creative ways to make it more delightful for her.

We each are motivated differently when it comes to the marriage bed. Ladies, your husband is pleased when you are intentional about lovemaking and enjoy it yourself, when you express admiration of him as a husband and as a man, when you delight in his body, and when you create adventure and variety in lovemaking. One inquiring wife posed this question to her husband, "What three things can I do to encourage you as a lover?" His prompt and succinct response was, "Be available and agreeable and be interested."[4]

Men, your wife finds the marriage bed delightful when there is trust and emotional intimacy between the two of you, when there is respect and open communication, and when non-sexual affection is expressed both in and out of the marriage bed. C. J. Mahaney, President of Sovereign Grace Ministries, reminds husbands, "In order for romance to deepen, you must touch the heart and mind of your wife before you touch her body."[5] You will spur her on with your generous love, acceptance, praise, and appreciation. She needs to feel safe with you.

STUMBLING BLOCKS TO GREAT SEX

If you believe all that you see on the movie screen or read in romance novels, everybody is having great sex. However, those of us still grounded in the real world know it's not always a dance of perfection. Even with the best of intentions, our lovemaking sometimes stumbles, falls flat, or never gets off the ground.

Here are some common obstacles for wives:

- Poor body image due to weight gain, surgical changes, or the expectations of society and her husband.

- Tiredness, fatigue, and the demands of work and home.

- Painful memories of sexual abuse.

- Distracted by stressed relationships and emotions.

- Feeling disconnected from her spouse due to plain inattention.

- Fear of rejection.

- The physical influence of hormones, thyroid changes, and medications.

Men are not immune to the challenges of lovemaking. Here are some obstacles husbands must confront:

- Making love less frequently than he likes.

- The impact of pornography and sexual addiction.

- His wife's apathy and indifference about lovemaking.

- Guilt from past sexual experiences.

- Lack of erotic visual stimulation from his wife.

- No variety or adventure in lovemaking initiated by his wife.

- Little admiration and affirmation from his wife for who he is, and for his best efforts to be a great husband and lover.

In addition to these, Scott Stanley, author of *A Lasting Promise,* warns about two types of anxiety that creep into the marriage bed – performance anxiety and relationship anxiety.[6] Performance anxiety is the result of too much concern about how good a job you are doing when you make love. You wonder if you're as good as the guy in the last romantic movie you watched, or as good as your spouse's previous sexual partners, if any.

Keeping an eye on your performance puts distance between you and your spouse. You focus on how you are doing rather than on being in the experience with your mate. The focus is no longer on the pleasure you are sharing. You simply can't be anxious and pleasantly aroused at the same time. This leads to common sexual troubles – premature ejaculation, maintaining an erection, and difficulty reaching orgasm.

Relationship anxiety comes from mishandled conflicts. Poorly handled marital conflict adds a layer of tension that affects everything else in the relationship. Your physical intimacy is probably more vulnerable to the effects of conflict and resentment than any other area.

David Olsen observes, "A marriage that is characterized by a lack of trust, that is stressed with financial concerns, or that is plagued with destructive conflict is probably not sexually satisfying for either partner."[7]

You can handle conflicts with good open discussions, a healthy resolution of problems, and keeping short accounts. The positive communication and forgiveness tools in your marital tool bag will come in handy here. It's critical to keep problems and disagreements off limits when you have the time to be together for touching or making love.

FROM GOOD TO GREAT IN THE MARRIAGE BED

In a scene from an old Woody Allen movie (*Annie Hall*), a marriage counselor separately questions a husband and wife. The counselor asks the wife, "How often do you and your husband have sex?" She responds, "Almost always. Three times a week." The counselor is then shown asking the husband, "How often do you and your wife have sex?" The husband responds, "Almost never. Three times a week."

Most spouses do not have the same need for physical affection and sexual intimacy. Typically, one desires to make love more frequently than the other one does. There is nothing wrong with that. Additionally, the man is not always the one who has the need for greater frequency. A young husband wrote, "Our sexual adjustment is very good, but my dear wife seems to have no idea that there are limits to a man's interest in sex. The few times I have tried to signal her to slow things down she seemed confused and hurt. Sex is great, but how do I introduce some moderation into the proceedings?" Many men reading this probably wonder why this guy is complaining.

Instead of fighting about frequency, you can practice *The Principle of Satisfaction* by honoring your spouse's desire for sexual intimacy. Your spouse will be happy, which means you will be happy. This is not to suggest that he or she can make unreasonable demands of you. There will be times when sickness, fatigue, and the stresses of life will require a rain check.

Your level of satisfaction will also increase when you take the time to understand what affects your sexual relationship. Your spouse's lack of sexual desire may not have anything to do with you. As stated earlier, your natural desire for sexual union must get over some hurdles that keep you from the love life you both crave. Take time to communicate openly about what affects your love life. A complete medical checkup can be valuable. It will also be helpful for you to deal with emotional problems, past events and relationships, hurt feelings, bitterness, and poor self-image. Contact your pastor, a Christian counselor, or a mature couple to help you work through these matters.

Another positive thing you can do is to resolve major conflicts effectively, which will not give bitterness an opportunity to take root. Couples are often surprised how quickly their sex life deteriorates when love is lost in conflict and hatred. Your sexual intimacy can be a powerful reflection of how things are going in other areas of your relationship.

> *It's critical to keep problems and disagreements off limits when you have the time to be together for touching or making love.*

Sexual intimacy in marriage is enhanced when you communicate clearly and honestly about what you desire, and about what you like or do not like. Don't be embarrassed. Try some of your suggestions at a time when you are relaxed and do not feel rushed. You will need to be patient with each other. Remember, great sex is not about performance. It's about creating an emotional, physical, and spiritual bond in your marriage that cannot be shattered.

A DISCIPLINED LOVER

A great lover in a great marriage is a disciplined lover. Discipline may seem to be an odd character trait for a lover, and the opposite of playful, spontaneous, or creative. However, a lack of opportunity and priority sabotages the spontaneity of many married couples. Here are several ways in which you can be disciplined in your love life:

- *Make sexual intimacy a priority.* – This starts with a positive attitude about sex, and the determination to prevent the "stuff of life" from crowding in on this vital area of married life. Give your best time and energy to this important part of your marriage.

- *Plan for sexual activity with your spouse.* – You may even have to put in on your calendars! You can then allow for spontaneity in the atmosphere, place, timing, and technique.

- *Take care of your body and mind.* – Good physical, mental, and emotional health empower your lovemaking.

- *Say "yes" more frequently.* – Saying "no" can become a habit that prolongs sexual dissatisfaction. So, even when you are tired or you just don't feel like it, go ahead and take the plunge. Many have reported they were glad they did.

- *Structure your life in such a way that you can be rested, rather than tired.* – Take a nap in the afternoon or go to bed earlier at night. Maybe you need to reclaim some time on your calendar because you are overcommitted.

- *Plan uninterrupted times together where you are free from the stress and distractions of family and work.* – Couples who have children at home will greatly benefit from such times. Arrange for grandparents or friends to take care of your children, while you have a special overnight at a nearby hotel (or at your empty house).

- *Be creative in your love life.* – Initiate lovemaking at unexpected times and in unexpected places. Try new positions and techniques. You might even try being the "initiator" if your spouse usually gets things started.

- *Read a book together about how to have a healthy sexual relationship.* – There are several good ones listed in the Resource Section of this book.

- *Take more time to enjoy the lovemaking.* – It doesn't have to be a race against the clock. For many people, that means going to bed earlier.

- *Ask God to bless your love life.* – He is very interested in helping you create a life of passion, joy, and satisfaction. Because of your inherent differences, you need God's grace to create a fulfilling intimate relationship.

HIGH DIVIDENDS

Work, children, school, church, sports, and countless other worthy activities compete for our time and attention. Exhaustion and fatigue are the major contributors to a low-sex marriage. Our fast track schedules leave little time and energy to give, share, or receive.

If your marriage is important to you, it's important to make time for physical intimacy. The investment of time and energy in your love life will yield high dividends. You will feel closer, more relaxed, more connected, and more married. It's a way to express your love for each other. The things that you do to irritate each other will seem less annoying. It makes your spouse happy, which makes you happy. It makes you special to each other because it's something you do only with each other.

A mutually satisfying love life is a significant tool in building your great marriage. So, fuel the fires of your marital intimacy. Say *no* to some good things and *yes* to a great love life with your spouse.

 TOOL TIME FOR COUPLES

1. How do you spell *intimacy*? In other words, what activities or actions help you to connect emotionally and physically with your spouse? How are you similar and different? What are the challenges in your marriage caused by these differences and similarities?

2. Read 1 Corinthians 7:3-4 on page 142. Discuss the following questions with your spouse:

    ▪ What makes lovemaking delightful for you?

    ▪ What are the challenges to lovemaking in our marriage?

    ▪ How can we practice *The Principle of Satisfaction* in our marriage?

CHAPTER 10

Building a Great Marriage in Stormy Weather

There are times when marriage is great, and there are times when "for better or for worse" is worse than you ever imagined. Charlie knows. He is 61-years-old and has been married to Rita for ten years. It's a second marriage for both of them and they are miserable. Nothing seems to be going right. Charlie was laid off from a very good job about three years after they were married. It took him nine months to get another job, but he had to take a substantial cut in pay and benefits. Rita is angry and bitter because she had to go back to work.

They have been to three different marriage counselors and found some help. However, Rita would find something wrong with the counselor and stop going. Eventually, they returned to their old ways of relating. Charlie knows that he should want to fix things, but he has no interest in his wife anymore. He says, "She constantly criticizes me and

I find myself hurling insults at her. She has so many hoops I must jump through for any sexual involvement, and I've decided I'm just not interested in trying to meet all her demands."

Charlie and Rita are beginning to talk about going their separate ways. They don't want to divorce, but they don't know what else to do.

> *You don't have to be married long before stormy weather attempts to capsize your marriage boat.*

Many, if not all, married couples have had their friendship stretched. You don't have to be married long before stormy weather attempts to capsize your marriage boat. Some have endured earth-shaking blows. I've walked with parents through the heartbreak of a child's premature death. I've seen couples suffer through business difficulties and job losses, repeated illnesses, marital infidelity, aging, mid-life crises, problems with aging parents, teenage rebellion, the death of parents, financial setbacks, grown children getting divorces, and children disgracing their family's name, just to name a few. The difficulties produced strength in many, while others never seemed to recover.

God is gracious and does not often allow couples to experience the same kind of suffering as Job did in the Bible. However, he does allow measured doses of trouble at sovereignly ordained intervals. The storms are different for each couple, but no less demanding.

FACING OUR OWN STORM

Cindy and I faced our own storm on a chilling December night in 1990. I stood in a hospital room similar to other times in my vocation as a pastor. However, this was different. This night, this room, this hospital, was about to find a permanent place in my memory. Cindy, the receiver of my promise of persevering love, occupied that hospital bed.

Seven months of unexplained numbness, pain and increasing discomfort preceded this hospital stay. A dozen guesses at the cause, vials of blood for evaluation, electrodes and pin pricks for tests, physical therapy to manage the pain – all added up to nothing. The doctors were perplexed. That was not very reassuring. We were happy to know what it was not, but frustrated because Cindy was losing more and more of her mobility. We prayed and persevered, trusting God for an answer.

The months before Cindy's hospitalization had gradually changed our home, our lifestyle, and our relationships. She was losing the ability to function independently in her daily life. Our daughters, ages 13 and 9 at the time, patiently and lovingly assumed more household duties. I found it difficult to add more duties to an already crowded calendar. The daily and weekly functions that Cindy administered and executed with such expertise had been taken for granted. The necessity of crutches for walking, the swelling of her legs when she would sit up, the inability to remain at our family table for the complete meal, and the restless nights of interrupted sleep were all draining energy from our family.

I felt so weak when she would look to me for help. What more could I do? Like many husbands, I approach problems with a "fix it" mentality. Often I was able to correct and repair whatever troubled my wife. However, what could I do about this? I did pray. I also drove her to doctor's appointments and the numerous diagnostic procedures. I held her when she cried tears of pain, anger, and frustration. It did not seem to be enough though.

None of this was fair, I reasoned. There was much to do for God – people to see, sermons to preach, seminars to lead, books to read, and articles to write. Nevertheless, my marital promise to love "in sickness and in health" was getting an Olympic workout. This stay in the hospital had not been on the itinerary when we were married in 1972. Yet, here we were. The last possible diagnostic test was complete. Now we waited for the doctor's report. Was it a brain tumor? Or would he once again say he had found nothing?

The verdict was in. Through a process of elimination, the doctor arrived at his diagnosis – Multiple Sclerosis (MS), a neurological disease, the cause of which is yet undetermined and there is no cure. It attacks the coating or insulation around the message-carrying nerve fibers in the brain and spinal cord causing varying interruptions of the nervous system.[1] Cindy released a declaration of praise to God with the announcement, which surprised the doctor and me. He reminded her of the seriousness of MS, but she said, "At least I'm not dying from a brain tumor."

WHY DOES GOD ALLOW STORMY WEATHER?

On my ride home from the hospital I prayed, "Thank you, God, for an answer. Not knowing has been awful. Thank you that it is not life threatening. But why MS? Why us?"

Those are tough questions. They are monsters and there are no easy answers. I used to tell people, "Don't ask *why*; but, ask *how* you can glorify God in this." As I faced my own unexplainable storm, I needed some answers.

Intellectually, I know that God is good, but this storm challenged my faith in God's goodness towards His children. A friend of mine wrestles with the same thing as he watches his wife battle cancer in her body. He regularly prays for her healing, but the cancer continues to be a threat to the marriage they are building. He wants to know what God is doing about it, because it is out of his control.

I don't presume to understand fully the mind and heart of God; however, I needed to get some answers that would help me stabilize the shifting sands beneath my feet. One thing I discovered was that stormy weather could be God's way of getting your attention about an area of your marriage, or personal life, which needs some work. God sometimes lets us experience the full consequences of our own unhealthy and unwise choices in order to get our attention.

Tom and Mary lived through some turbulent years in their marriage. Fear of Tom's anger led Mary to keep information from him. Tom knew his work schedule interfered with his marriage, but he continued to work at the same pace. Other bad choices included using sex as a reward system rather than as an expression of intimacy, and not being truthful about their financial debt. Instead of taking responsibility for bad choices and turning toward each other in love, they fell into a pattern of fear, shame, and blame which compounded the difficulties they faced.

> *God sometimes lets us experience the full consequences of our own unhealthy and unwise choices in order to get our attention.*

I eventually discovered another reason for our storm – to give us a ministry to others. The Apostle Paul wrote to the Corinthian Christians about a stormy time in his life, a time when he thought he would die in the middle of his troubles. He found comfort and deliverance in God, which led to these words of praise:

> *Praise be to the God and Father of our Lord Jesus Christ, the Father of compassion and the God of all comfort, who comforts us in all our troubles, so that we can comfort those in any trouble with the comfort we ourselves have received from God. – 2 Corinthians 1:3-4*

What we have learned about God's grace and comfort in our marriage has opened doors of opportunity that otherwise would have been closed to us. The first hint of this came four months after Cindy was diagnosed with MS. I spoke at a marriage retreat in New Hampshire and explained to the group what we had experienced over the course of several months. I told them that Cindy would not be joining me at the retreat until Saturday afternoon. As soon as the session ended, a couple approached me and asked for some time to talk. The wife said, "I hope Cindy will be able to come. I was just diagnosed with MS and I need to talk to somebody about it." We carved out a chunk of time on Saturday night to sit with this couple and encourage them with the lessons we were learning about God's comfort. I have lost track of how many similar conversations we have had over the years.

Our message about strong marriages and families is strengthened because of our storm.

Our message about resilient marriages and families is more real because of our storm. Does that mean that we don't want God to end the storm? Of course not, but we are not embittered by the storm. We know that God is redeeming it for his glory.

ANCHOR DEEP

What can a couple do to protect their marriage in the middle of a storm? I heard about a man who had just bought a boat and kept it in a harbor on the coast of Florida. A hurricane was brewing just off the coast and was about to hit land. He did not know what to do. He had made a sizable investment in this boat and he did not want to lose it. A friend, who had experience with both boats and hurricanes, gave him this advice, "Don't attempt to tie the boat to the dock or anything on land. It will be torn to pieces. Your only hope is to anchor deep. Take four anchors and drop them deep. The boat will be able to ride out the storm."

There is wise counsel in that story for those of us who must build our marriages in stormy weather. We must find at least four anchors that will keep us from being torn apart. Here are the four anchors that have helped us:

Anchor #1: Trust God – Writing to the first century Christians about how to deal with difficult times, the Apostle Peter commanded, "Humble yourselves, therefore, under God's mighty hand, that he may lift you up in due time. Cast all your anxiety on him because he cares for you" (1Peter 5:6-7). To keep our marriage from crashing on the rocks, we daily submit to God's guidance for our lives and marriage. We trust that God knows what's best for us.

> *God has marked out for each of us a path that is leading to unparalleled joy for us, and glory for him.*

Over the years, I have come to understand that life is not fair, but God is always good. The indispensable basis for my enduring, unwavering, and joyful commitment to building a great marriage in stormy weather is an implicit faith in God's goodness. I stake my life on the certain truth that God would never ask us, his children, to go through anything that does not have our well being in view. God has marked out for each of us a path that is leading to unparalleled joy for us, and glory for him.

Anchor #2: Love Each Other Deeply – In stormy weather, give top priority to maintaining a loving relationship with each other. You may be tempted to turn away from one another. Don't! Instead, turn toward each other to provide a shelter in the storm.

This anchor is based on these words from the Bible, "Above all, love each other deeply, because love covers over a multitude of sins" (1 Peter 4:8). The word, "deeply," comes from a Greek word that means, "to stretch out," as a runner stretches out to cross the finish line at the end of a race. The application in marriage is that each spouse stretches to the maximum to ride out the storm together. You aggressively make your relationship with your spouse a priority during times of strain and struggle, and you keep doing the things that express love and friendship – fun dates, casual walks, and meaningful conversations.

Your commitment to love deeply is of utmost importance. Some believe that a great marriage is a 50/50 partnership. I do not. You each need to be prepared to give 100% of yourself to make this marriage strong, healthy, and enduring. There may be days when one of you can only give 40%, but the other one will be there giving 100%. Newspaper columnist Robert Brown, in comparing sports and marriage, wrote, "In sports, you can't always get everyone on the team to give their best all the time, so the rest of the players need to be playing at the top of their game to compensate for anyone who falls back."[2] One of the great privileges of marriage is that we do not have to go through these stormy times alone. God has provided a partner with whom we can share the pain of the process.

Anchor #3: Let God Shape You – When I announced to our church family that Cindy had been diagnosed with Multiple Sclerosis, there was an outpouring of compassionate and sympathetic words. I have forgotten most of them, but this one remains, "I believe this will be the maturing of Willie Batson." I didn't know how to process those words at first. I thought I was quite mature at the time. However, God has used this storm in our marriage to show me how prideful and selfish I am. I have learned what James meant when he wrote, "Perseverance must finish its work so that you may be mature and complete, not lacking anything" (James 1:4). That must be what the author of *Sacred Marriage,* Gary Thomas, had in mind when he wrote, "If your marriage is tough, get down on your knees and thank God that he has given you an opportunity for unparalleled spiritual growth."[3] That's not easy to do unless you believe in the goodness of God.

I have also learned that God works through whatever happens, to bring about something redemptive for Christians who remain true to their calling. He uses stormy weather to shape and mold us into the image of Jesus Christ. The Apostle Paul wrote about this in his letter to the Christians in Rome:

> *God knew what he was doing from the very beginning. He decided from the outset to shape the lives of those who love him along the same lines as the life of his Son. The Son stands first in the line of humanity he restored. We see the original and intended shape of our lives there in him."* – Romans 8:29, MSG

When we choose to let God use our stormy times to shape us, our marriages will be anchored deep and able to ride out the storm. If we refuse to change, the anchor line will snap and our marriage boat will begin to flounder.

Anchor #4: Persevere in Faithfulness – In your marriage vows, you promised to remain faithful regardless of all the changes and adversities, regardless of good times, bad times, wealth or poverty. You promised to persevere with each other through the changing seasons of life. Some storms last longer and are bigger than others. The damage they cause can seem almost beyond repair.

In one of our ministry newsletters, I wrote about the challenge of living with a chronic disease in marriage. Several people responded with notes. One wrote, "Been there, done that, got the t-shirt…Yet, despite all the challenges, I wouldn't trade places." Another particularly stirring note came from Jay, whose parents have been friends of ours for many years.

> *My Dad is experiencing first hand what "in sickness and in health" really means. Mom is an advanced Alzheimer's patient now. Don't know how much time she has left, but she is basically unresponsive, can't walk, eat, or do any-thing to take care of herself. Dad, God love him, is caring for her 100% of the time. He's getting help from Hospice, but most of the work rests on his shoulders. He bathes her, dresses her, cooks all the meals, feeds her, lifts her in and out of her wheel chair, and tucks her into bed at night. I'm certain, that when he made those vows almost 60 years ago, he never expected that "in sickness and in health" would end up like this. He has had to give up most of his organ playing for the local churches to take care of her.*

Jay continued his note with a comment about the impact this is having on him.

> *From his son's perspective, what a great testimony he has become! Without even realizing it — that of all the other "things" he has done in the Lord's service over the course of his life, this would perhaps become his greatest achieve-ment — to lovingly care for and tend to his wife long after*

*the personal joy and gratitude for doing so had disap-
peared. I don't think she even knows who he is anymore.*

Gary Thomas wrote that marriage "may indeed be a difficult road, but it is a holy road that can lead us toward God."[4] I'm sure that Jay's father finds God's grace sufficient for each day he has with his wife. He is wholly devoted to her and their God. Others may not always see such faithful perseverance, but God does.

IT IS HARD

To keep your marriage from crashing on the rocks during a stormy period, you must be prepared to anchor deep with these four anchors. Your storm may not be a life-threatening or debilitating disease. It may be a loss of a different kind. The storm winds may be coming from within your own home as you wrestle with a child who is hanging out with the wrong crowd, doing drugs, and breaking all of the house rules. Financial debt beats you down. Addictions force you into shame and secrecy. Miscarriages or infertility frustrates your hope of becoming parents.

Living through stormy weather in marriage is not easy, even when you have put out these four anchors. The storm does not end simply because you put out the anchors. Riding out the storm can be hard, like reading highly technical books on theology or science or philosophy. Some pages of information are hard to comprehend. The only thing you can do is put a marker there and go on reading. Perhaps later it will make some sense.

What about the storms caused by abuse, addictions, and other sinful behaviors? Must a spouse persevere in such situations? The intensity of every situation is different, but my basic guidance is to seek the wise counsel of Godly people – your pastor or a professional counselor. No one should put himself or herself in harm's way in a marriage. A period of separation may be justified until the out-of-control spouse is ready to change his or her abusive and sinful behaviors.

WE'RE MOVING ON

My promise of commitment to one woman, "till death do us part," has weathered storms with gale force winds and a few bombing raids by enemy aircraft for more than three decades. I have developed respect for the marriage vows I made when it seemed nothing could go wrong. Cindy and I don't understand all that has happened to us, but we are moving on to build a great marriage that glorifies the God we love and serve.

He has blessed us with a growing love in the midst of these challenging days. There are limitations, but we are learning to adjust and thrive in God's grace. Again, I am encouraged by the author of *Sacred Marriage*, Gary Thomas, who writes, "Romantic love has no elasticity to it. It can never be stretched; it simply shatters. Mature love, the kind demanded of a good marriage, must stretch."[5]

God calls us to ride out the storms together for a greater purpose, a purpose bigger than our comfort and happiness in life.

God calls us to ride out the storms together for a greater purpose, a purpose bigger than our comfort and happiness in life. We have the opportunity to grow deeper into Christ, draw closer to each other, and show a pessimistic, cynical world the glorious strength of grace and faith. In a great marriage, two individuals unite under the grace of God to develop the capacity to go through the storm. Do not run from the storms in your marriage. Embrace them. Grow in them.

Draw near to God and each other because of them. A great marriage is not something you find. It is something you are determined to work for every moment God gives you together.

Romantic love has no elasticity to it. It can never be stretched; it simply shatters. Mature love, the kind demanded of a good marriage, must stretch.

Gary Thomas

 TOOL TIME FOR COUPLES

1. How have difficulties in your married life served as an instrument of growth for you individually and as a couple?

2. What storm are you and your spouse facing right now? How can each of the *anchors* mentioned in this chapter help you go through that storm?

   - *Trust God*

   - *Love Each Other Deeply*

   - *Let God Shape You*

   - *Persevere in Faithfulness*

3. What can you and your spouse do to protect your marriage from the destructive influence of hurts and difficulties? What is the first thing you will do this week?

Epilogue

You now have a set of tools that can help you build and maintain your great marriage. You must use them on a regular basis to keep your marriage running smoothly. Many people rarely think about improving their marriage unless it is in trouble. I've noticed a similarity between the way people take care of their marriages and the way they take care of their cars and trucks.

They Do Nothing, and Break Down. – There are people who ignore the preventative maintenance schedule of their automobiles. They disregard the odd rumbling sounds coming from underneath, and are convinced they have an adequate fuel supply, regardless of what the gas gauge says. Eventually, they break down by the side of the road and are towed to a service center.

The same thing happens to married people. You refuse to heed the warnings and lack the motivation or interest in preventing trouble. The next thing you know, your spouse drags you into a counselor's office or a marriage seminar as a means of repairing the problem. This is often costly, as it is when we neglect to take care of our vehicles. Years of neglect will require major changes in behavior and attitude.

They Wait Until They Get a Warning Ticket. – A police officer stopped me one night because a headlight bulb on my car had burned out. He gave me a warning ticket, which stated that I had a certain amount of time to correct the problem. I had hoped to be able to make it home without being stopped again. No such luck! About five miles from the first stop and in a different town, the now familiar flashing lights rolled up behind me. When I showed the officer the warning ticket from the other town, he laughed and said, "Must be a slow night." As I drove away, I wondered why I had not asked him to call ahead to the next town and let them know I had already been warned – not once, but twice. I made it home and took steps to replace the burned out light before the sun set the next day.

Some married people do not take the time to invest any energy in marital maintenance. It's the old adage, "If it ain't broke, don't fix it." They just keep going about their own agendas until something happens to get their attention. It may be an argument that leads to abuse, or a narrow escape from a sexual temptation, or a health-related issue that causes them to refocus their priorities. While not ideal, couples who wait until they get a warning ticket will often seek help. They will talk to a pastor or return to the positive patterns of relating, while others will attend a marriage class or seminar to stabilize their relationship.

They follow a preventative maintenance schedule. – Like those who zealously perform the preventative maintenance rituals upon their cars, there are couples who focus creative energy on their marriage as a means of preventing trouble. A husband once told me that for 30 years he made sure that his car's oil was changed regularly, that the tire pressure was kept at factory specifications, and that various fluid levels were maintained according to the owner's manual. It was not until after attending one of our marriage seminars that he realized that he had neglected to keep his marriage running smoothly through regular check-ups.

With a little preventative maintenance, you can save yourself a huge chunk of time and emotional energy trying to repair a big problem later on. It can make your marriage run smoother and be more fun in the years ahead. Couples who take this path have intentional discussions about how their marriage is going, read books together on how to improve communication, spend time having fun, and attend marriage enrichment events. Most married people will say that their marriage is important to them. The truth of that statement is seen in the care given to build a lasting marriage.

Your marriage may be a good marriage, but it can always be strengthened and improved. If you are serious about building a great marriage, I have included several items in the Resource Section to help you take care of your marriage. Look at them and decide together what you will do to keep on building your great marriage.

It is my hope that the tools in this book will help you build a great marriage, as an example and an encouragement to others. If you have found this book helpful, please share it with your friends who want to build a great marriage. I would be happy to hear about your progress (www.familybuilders.net).

Notes

Chapter 1: "A Marital Tool Bag"

1. David Augsburger, *Cherishable: Love and Marriage* (Herald Press, 1971).

Chapter 2: "Build a Great Marriage on a Great Foundation"

1. Gary L. Thomas, *Devotions for a Sacred Marriage* (Zondervan Publishers, 2005), 12.
2. Riette Woods, *Prayers for a Strong Marriage* (www.praymag.com, 2007).
3. Charles Sell, *Achieving the Impossible - Intimate Marriage* (Multnomah Press, 1982), 155.

Chapter 3: "Become the Host in Your Marriage"

1. From an article by Jim Killam, *What Does It Do For Me?* (Marriage Partnership, Summer 2005).
2. Cecil Osborne, *The Art of Understanding Your Mate*, (Zondervan, 1988), 88.
3. From an article by Jim Mueller, *Strategic Romance* on the Growthtrac website: www.growthtrac.com
4. From an article by Marti Attoun, that appeared on the website: https://www.americanprofile.com/article/5155.html
5. Adapted from *Starved for Affection: Why We Crave It, How to Get It, and Why It's Important in Marriage*, Randy Carlson (Tyndale House Publishers, 2005).
6. Gary Thomas, *Sacred Marriage* (Zondervan Publishing, 2000), 190.
7. Gordon MacDonald, *Magnificent Marriage* (Tyndale House, 1976), 129.
8. Although I heard this story in a seminar, you can read more about this in Dr. Chapman's book, *Covenant Marriage* (Broadman and Holman Publishers, 2003).

Chapter 4: "What's Love Got to Do With It?"

1. Robert J. Sternberg, *The Triangle of Love: Intimacy, Passion, Commitment* (Basic Books, 1988).
2. Gary D. Chapman, *The Five Love Languages* (Northfield Publishing, 1992), 30.
3. Elizabeth Barrett Browning, *How Do Love Thee? (Sonnet 43)*, found on the website: www.poets.org/viewmedia.php/prmMID/15384
4. Gary Thomas, *Devotions for a Sacred Marriage* (Zondervan Publishing, 2005), 100.
5. Lance Armstrong, with Sally Jenkins, *Every Second Counts* (Doubleday, 2003).
6. Emerson Eggerichs, *Love & Respect*, (Integrity Publishers, 2004), 49.
7. Eggerichs, 32.
8. Adapted from information on this website: http://www.buzzle.com/editorials/3-16-2005-67161.asp
9. Adapted from information on the website: www.wd40.com

Chapter 5: "Help! We're From Different Worlds"

1. Harold L. Myra, *Conan or Cosby*, Marriage Partnership (Spring 1988), 48.
2. Gary D. Chapman, *The Five Love Languages* (Northfield Publishing, 1992).
3. Walter Wangerin, *As For Me And My House* (Thomas Nelson, 1989), 44.
4. Paul Tournier, *To Understand Each Other* (Westminster John Knox Press, 1976), 42.
5. "But God demonstrates his own love for us in this: While we were still sinners, Christ died for us." (Romans 5:8)
6. Francine Klagsbrun, *Married People: Staying Together in the Age of Divorce* (Bantam Books, 1985).

Chapter 6: "Tools for Great Communication"

1. *Bits & Pieces*, March 4, 1993, p. 23.
2. David H. Olson and Amy K. Olson, *Empowering Couples: Building on Your Strengths* (Life Innovations, Inc., 2000), p. 26.
3. Les Parrott and Leslie Parrott, *Your Time-Starved Marriage* (Zondervan, 2006), 35.
4. Parrott and Parrott, 98.
5. Parrott and Parrott, 39.

6. Based on a story told by Dr. Richard Selzer in *A Second Chicken Soup for the Woman's Soul: 101 More Stories to Open*, Jack Canfield (HCI, 1996).
7. Les Parrott and Leslie Parrott, *Love Talk* (Zondervan, 2004), 125.
8. Dwight Small, *After You've Said I Do* (Fleming H. Revell, 1968), 81.

Chapter 7: "You Spent How Much?"

1. Crown Financial Ministries (www.crown.org); Dave Ramsey Ministries (www.daveramsey.com)
2. David H. Olson and Amy K. Olson, *Empowering Couples: Building on Your Strengths* (Life Innovations, Inc., 2000), 97.
3. Olson and Olson, 98.
4. The main principles are roughly based on a sermon I heard by Rick Warren. I have added additional thoughts and ideas.
5. Dave Ramsey, *How to Communicate with Your Spouse about Money*, www.daveramsey.com.
6. Olson and Olson, p. 98.
7. Olson and Olson, p. 99.
8. Russ Crosson, *Money and Your Marriage* (Word Publishing, 1989), 204.
9. Crosson, p. 12.

Chapter 8: "Ground Rules for a Fair Fight"

1. Gary Thomas, *Sacred Marriage*, 162.
2. From an email I received from Tommy Nelson, *Why Revenge is a Bad Idea*, (October 13, 2004).
3. Gary Smalley, *The DNA of Relationships* (Tyndale House Publishers, 2004), 153ff.
4. Smalley, *The DNA of Relationships*, 156.
5. Smalley, *The DNA of Relationships*, 40-43.
6. John Gottman, *The Seven Principles for Making Marriage Work* (Three Rivers Press, 1999), 28.
7. Gary and Barbara Rosberg, *Divorce-Proof Your Marriage* (Tyndale House, 2002), 257.
8. Evelyn and James Whitehead, *A Sense of Sexuality: Christian Love and Intimacy* (Doubleday, 1989), 197.
9. Gary Thomas, *Sacred Marriage*, 170.
10. Lewis B. Smedes, *The Art of Forgiveness* (Random House, 1996), 177-178.
11. David Stoop, *Experiencing God Together – Spiritual Intimacy in Marriage* (Tyndale House Publishers, 1996), 145.
12. For more on Biblical reconciliations see: Matthew 5:23-24; 18:15-17; Colossians 3:12-13.

13. Gary Chapman and Jennifer Thomas, *The Five Languages of Apology* (Northfield Publishing, 2006).

Chapter 9: "Great Sex in a Great Marriage"

1. David H. Olson and Amy K. Olson, *Empowering Couples: Building on Your Strengths* (Life Innovations, Inc., 2000), 124.
2. Olson and Olson, 125.
3. Thomas, *Sacred Marriage*, 206-207
4. Joseph and Linda Dillow and Peter and Lorraine Pintus, *Intimacy Ignited* (NavPress, 2004), 235.
5. C. J. Mahaney, *Sex, Romance, and the Glory of God* (Crossway Books, 2004), 28.
6. Scott Stanley, *A Lasting Promise* (Jossey-Bass Publishers, 1998), 251-255.
7. Olson and Olson, 123.

Chapter 10: "Building a Great Marriage in Stormy Weather"

1. For more information about Multiple Sclerosis, visit the website of the National Society for Multiple Sclerosis (www.nationalmssociety.org).
2. Robert Brown, *Marriage, Athletics Take a Lot of Work* (Carroll County Times – Maryland, April 6, 2008).
3. Thomas, *Sacred Marriage*, 129.
4. Thomas, *Devotions for a Sacred Marriage*, 117.
5. Thomas, *Sacred Marriage*, 15-16.

Your Marriage Checkup (Husband)

(To be completed before and after reading the book.)

Individually, choose your level of satisfaction in the following general categories of your marriage. Then, discuss the questions below with your spouse.

AREAS OF YOUR MARRIAGE	DISSATISFIED								SATISFIED	
Financial Management	1	2	3	4	5	6	7	8	9	10
Companionship	1	2	3	4	5	6	7	8	9	10
Spiritual Growth	1	2	3	4	5	6	7	8	9	10
Communication	1	2	3	4	5	6	7	8	9	10
Leisure Activities	1	2	3	4	5	6	7	8	9	10
Friends & Extended Family	1	2	3	4	5	6	7	8	9	10
Community & Church Activities	1	2	3	4	5	6	7	8	9	10
Parenting	1	2	3	4	5	6	7	8	9	10
Romance & Intimacy	1	2	3	4	5	6	7	8	9	10
Household Responsibilities	1	2	3	4	5	6	7	8	9	10
Conflict Resolution	1	2	3	4	5	6	7	8	9	10
Sexual Fulfillment	1	2	3	4	5	6	7	8	9	10

1. What are the best aspects of your marriage?

2. What are the areas that cause the greatest stress in your marriage?

3. What are you going to do during the next 90 days to build on the best aspects of your marriage and minimize the areas that cause the greatest stress in your marriage?

Your Marriage Checkup (Wife)

(To be completed before and after reading the book.)

Individually, choose your level of satisfaction in the following general categories of your marriage. Then, discuss the questions below with your spouse.

AREAS OF YOUR MARRIAGE	DISSATISFIED									SATISFIED
Financial Management	1	2	3	4	5	6	7	8	9	10
Companionship	1	2	3	4	5	6	7	8	9	10
Spiritual Growth	1	2	3	4	5	6	7	8	9	10
Communication	1	2	3	4	5	6	7	8	9	10
Leisure Activities	1	2	3	4	5	6	7	8	9	10
Friends & Extended Family	1	2	3	4	5	6	7	8	9	10
Community & Church Activities	1	2	3	4	5	6	7	8	9	10
Parenting	1	2	3	4	5	6	7	8	9	10
Romance & Intimacy	1	2	3	4	5	6	7	8	9	10
Household Responsibilities	1	2	3	4	5	6	7	8	9	10
Conflict Resolution	1	2	3	4	5	6	7	8	9	10
Sexual Fulfillment	1	2	3	4	5	6	7	8	9	10

1. What are the best aspects of your marriage?

2. What are the areas that cause the greatest stress in your marriage?

3. What are you going to do in the next 90 days to build on the best aspects of your marriage and minimize the areas that cause the greatest stress in your marriage?

Taking Care of Your Marriage

1. Compliment your spouse daily. Don't take each other for granted.

2. Initiate a stress-reducing conversation with your spouse at the end of each day.

3. Plan a weekly relaxing, low-pressure activity for you and your spouse that will build your marital friendship. Make positive connection a priority as you intentionally schedule regular time for fun, friendship, and sensuality in your marriage. Be sure to protect these times from conflict and the need to deal with issues. Marital research tells us that anything that increases the amount of time a couple spends together will increase their level of marital satisfaction.

4. Hold a weekly Marriage Meeting. This is not a date night. It's like a staff meeting to help you stay connected with each other and deal with any issues that may come up. You only need about 30–45 minutes and it's best to schedule it for the same day each week. A sample agenda for this meeting is included in this Resource Section. If you miss a week, don't give up. Just pick it up the next week.

5. Plan a quarterly mini-marriage retreat away from home, using this time for fun and for evaluating your relationship. You may want to use the online Family Builders *Couples Checkup* inventory on this retreat. An easy and enjoyable online tool, it helps you identify your relational strengths and talk about areas that need more growth. Visit the Family Builders Ministries' website for more details (www.familybuilders.net).

6. Sign up for daily email marriage tips that inspire you to build a great marriage. Family Builders Ministries has an email program that correlates with this book (www.familybuilders.net).

7. Annually attend a marriage enrichment conference where you can spend significant time with each other talking about how to improve and protect your marriage. The Family Builders Ministries' website (www.familybuilders.net) includes listings of conferences and links to other organizations that sponsor marriage enrichment events.

A Preventative Maintenance Plan for Your Marriage

1. (Individually) On a separate sheet of paper, list one thing you want to do to improve your marriage for each of the time periods below:

    a. Daily

    b. Weekly

    c. Monthly

    d. Quarterly

    e. Yearly

2. (Together) Compare your answers with your spouse's answers. What are the similarities? How can you negotiate the differences?

3. (Together) Now decide on what you want to do for each of the time periods listed. Write them on a separate sheet of paper. This becomes your marital preventative maintenance plan for the coming 12 months. Post it in a place where it will remind you of how you have decided to build a great marriage.

The Marriage Meeting Agenda
(This is a couple meeting held weekly at a regular time.)

■ Devotional times for the week
   (Schedule "when" and "what" for you as a couple and/or a family)

■ Greatest joy of the week
   (Personally; does not have to be marriage related)

■ Greatest struggle of the week
   (Personally; does not have to be marriage related)

■ An affirmation
   (A positive statement about your spouse)

■ A wish or a hope
   (For your family/marriage/life)

■ Prayer
   (This is a way to close your time together. Take turns praying. Give thanks
   for each other and pray for your marriage, children, and other topics that may
   have come up during the meeting.)

Suggested Reading for Further Marriage Growth

- *10 Great Dates to Energize Your Marriage* by David and Claudia Arp (Zondervan Publishing House)

- *A Lasting Promise* – Scott Stanley, Daniel Trathen, Savanna McCain, and Milt Bryan (Jossey-Bass Publishers)

- *Divorce-Proof Your Marriage* by Gary and Barbara Rosberg (Tyndale House Publishers)

- *Experiencing God Together – Spiritual Intimacy in Marriage* by David Stoop (Tyndale House Publishers)

- *I Love You More* by Les and Leslie Parrott (Zondervan Publishing House)

- *Intimacy Ignited* by Joseph and Linda Dillow and Peter and Lorraine Pintus,(NavPress)

- *Love & Respect* by Dr. Emerson Eggerichs (Integrity Publishers)

- *Men Are Like Waffles, Women Are Like Spaghetti* by Bill Farrel and Pam Ferral (Harvest Publishers)

- *Sacred Marriage* by Gary Thomas (Zondervan)

- *Sex, Romance, and the Glory of God* by C. J. Mahaney (Crossway Books)

- *Sheet Music* by Kevin Leman (Tyndale House Publishers)

- *The DNA of Relationships* by Gary Smalley (Tyndale House Publishers)

- *The Five Languages of Apology* by Gary Chapman and Jennifer Thomas (Northfield Publishing)

- *The Five Love Languages* by Gary D. Chapman (Northfield Publishing)

- *The Second Half of Marriage* by David and Claudia Arp (Zondervan Publishing House)

ABOUT THE AUTHOR

 William (*Willie*) Batson, MAFM, is the Founder and President of Family Builders Ministries, Inc., an organization dedicated to serving married couples, parents, and those who minister to them. Willie and his wife, Cindy, were married in 1972, after meeting at a Christian college in New England. They are the parents of two married daughters and recently became grandparents.

Willie is an ordained pastor with an undergraduate degree in theology from Berkshire Christian College and a Master of Arts in Family Ministry from Gordon-Conwell Theological Seminary. He has served churches in South Carolina, Connecticut, New Hampshire, and Maine. Additionally, he is a trainer for the *Prepare/Enrich Inventories* by Life Innovations, Inc. and a charter member of the American Association of Christian Counselors.

With a passionate desire to help couples and parents fulfill God's plan for the family, Willie founded Family Builders Ministries in 1987, while still a local church pastor. Thousands of married couples and families have been strengthened through the teaching and training of Family Builders Ministries. As a result, many congregations have renewed their focus on the family and are developing creative and effective ways in which to address the needs of today's family.

*Due to a busy schedule, Willie cannot provide individual or couple counseling.

Family Builders Ministries is a 501(c)(3) faith-based nonprofit organization dedicated to serving married couples, parents, and those who minister to them.

PURPOSE
To transform hearts and homes through of Jesus Christ.

PASSION
To serve Jesus Christ by equipping people for great marriages and families from generation to generation.

VISION
To see every married couple and every parent living in authentic, healthy relationships as a means of transforming hearts and homes.

MISSION
To provide opportunities and tools that couples, parents, and those who minister to them can use in building great marriages and families from generation to generation.

Family Builders Ministries is a donor-supported ministry. We invite you to join us as a supporting partner in this mission to build great marriages and families from generation to generation. Please contact us for more information.

FAMILY BUILDERS MINISTRIES

Rev. William Batson, MAFM – Founder/President
PO Box 274 – Cape Neddick, ME 03902-0274 – Phone: (207) 361-1030
Email: info@familybuilders.net – Web site: www.familybuilders.net

Building Great Marriages & Families...from Generation to Generation

SEMINARS FOR COUPLES

This is our flagship marriage seminar, designed to help couples identify the qualities of a lasting love and friendship. Session topics include: *Help! We're from Different Worlds; Ground Rules for Communication; The Art of Making Love; and How Do We Stay Friends?*

This fun and right-to-the-point marriage seminar explores ways in which couples deepen the passion and intimacy of their relationship. Using the beautiful love story in Song of Solomon, each session is filled with practical help on how married couples can express and receive love in marriage.

A car needs attention when the engine backfires, the brakes squeal, and the warning lights refuse to dim. Like a car, marriages need consistent upkeep to stay running at peak performance. This seminar uses the Family Builders Couple's Checkup to provide the preventive maintenance every marriage needs.

SEMINARS FOR PARENTS

This parenting seminar will demonstrate how parents can develop healthy parenting skills that will be a blessing to their children. They will determine whether their home environment is helping or hindering the process of passing the baton of faith to their children.

This parenting seminar will assist parents who care about raising children who will love Jesus and want to live their lives for Him. Becoming intentional about spiritual training at home may create a knot of tension in the stomach due to past failure or intimidation. However, this seminar encourages parents to start fresh and develop a passion for the most important task of Christian parenting.

SEMINARS FOR LEADERS

This practical and relevant seminar can help mobilize your congregation to give direction, healing, and hope to marriages and families. You will learn a systematic plan for building a great marriage and family ministry in the local church.

This seminar is designed to train couples from your church with the required skills and tools for mentoring couples and for recruiting and training other marriage mentors. They will discover a marriage-mentoring model that can be used in small groups and couple-to-couple mentoring. Learn from those who are experienced in mentoring other couples and leading marriage ministries in their churches.

SEMINAR FOR A MEN'S RETREAT

Loving God and loving others – have those loves been weak or missing in your life? The focus in this stirring weekend is the Great Commandment of Jesus: "Love the Lord your God with all your heart and with all your soul and with all your mind" (Matthew 22:37). Your heart is the innermost part of your being that God has uniquely designed to do all things in accordance with His will. It is the measure of your integrity – the measure of who you are as a man.

Our seminars are typically one-day events hosted by local churches, but they can be adapted for a full weekend retreat. They feature a practical Bible-based presentation, interactive activities, and time for reflection and decision-making. We are flexible and will be happy to work with you on all of the hosting details. Finances for a seminar are reasonable. Contact us to discuss these arrangements and to reserve a weekend.

Email: info@familybuilders.net

HEALTHY MARRIAGE TIPS EMAIL

At Family Builders Ministries, we are keenly aware of the challenges couples face in keeping their relationship strong and healthy. Rev. William Batson, Founder/ President of Family Builders Ministries, often tells the story of Lance Armstrong, seven-time winner of the Tour de France, who wrote about his failed marriage: "We forgot to do the most important thing. We forgot to be married."

To help married couples focus on their marriages, Family Builders Ministries is offering a 30-day e-coaching course on building a healthy marriage. It's very simple. We want to send you 30 easy but powerful marriage-building tips. Each day, for 30 days, you will receive by email an idea that you can put into practice that day.

It's simple and it's free! All you have to do is sign up at our website (www.familybuilders.net). Don't delay. Sign up and be ready to see your marriage flourish with God's help. After you sign up, tell your friends about this wonderful opportunity.

"COUPLE CHECKUP" CAN BRING NEW LIGHT TO YOUR MARRIAGE

The *Family Builders' Couple Checkup* is an easy and enjoyable way for engaged and married couples to learn about each other and bring more intimacy into their relationship. By assessing 20 key relationship areas, it helps couples identify their relationship strengths and discuss areas that need more growth.

The confidential Couple Checkup is available online at the Family Builders web site (www.familybuilders.net). After completing the checkup, couples download a confidential report that will give feedback about how they each view their relationship. A 24-page discussion guide is also provided. Powered by PREPARE-ENRICH, these assessments have been trusted by over two-million couples & 60,000 counselors worldwide. The cost is $29.95 per couple, but the results are priceless.